Stephen Gaskin is an American hippy philosopher. In the 1960's he taught Monday Night Class every week for five years to the emerging counterculture in San Francisco. In 1971, Stephen and 250 others founded the Farm, in Summertown, Tennessee, which now includes 2,000 people in a dozen branches around the world.

Mind at Play is a collection of essays on religion, politics, philosophy and current affairs, in which Stephen applies the vision gained from building a telepathic community to the problems of contemporary society.

The earliest days of tripping taught the essential philosophy behind *Mind at Play*, centered around truth and compassion, and the fundamental equality of all the people. The lesson also included the sanctity of life force, and the necessity to recognize and respect that which is Holy.

From this point of view, Stephen discusses international politics, multinational corporations, religious cults, nuclear power, non-violence, and the preservation of a natural way of life in today's technological society.

From Marshal McLuhan and the media to friendly expositions of Zen and Christianity, from global excursions of mind to an analysis of international health care plans, *Mind at Play* offers a fresh viewpoint on the state of the planet, and on human behavior.

mind at play

mind at play

by Stephen Gaskin

The Book Publishing Company
Summertown, Tennessee 38483

Library of Congress Card No: 79-91244

Publisher: Paul Mandelstein
Editor: Matthew McClure
Production Manager: Jane Ayers
Artwork: David Long (cover), Bonnie Kaufman, Gregory Lowrey, James Hartman
Composing: Matthew McClure, Jane Ayers, Carolyn James, Suzanne Suarez, Lil Leighton
Layout: Tortesa Livick, James Egan
Darkroom: Daniel Luna, Valerie Epstein, Nancy Van Camp
Lithography: Jeffrey Clark, Thomas Malamed-Durocher, Katherine Nestler
Printing and Production: Robert Seidenspinner, John Seward, Richard Martin, Albert Livick, Andrew Nestler, Keith Martin, David Prentice, David Stitz, Martell Ray, Marilyn Dunning

Family Tree photo courtesy of Uncle Ted Thomas

ISBN 0-913990-24-8

Table of Contents

Free Will and a Fair Shake

One of the political officers here in Lewis County told me that he had never intended to go into politics, but he looked and he saw that this one man was going to run for this office, and he'd known the man for forty years. He felt it was the least he could do, to step forward and take that office. And that's sort of how I got into this racket. I was minding my own business on Haight Street, quietly trying to blow my mind, and I heard a bunch of teachers come out telling the folks a bunch of teachings, and a lot of it was so dumb and so superstitious and so destructive and so backward and un-teaching-from-reality, that I felt the least I could do was to step forward and start talking.

And it's become infinitely more complex since then. But sometimes I think there was such an incredible clear shaft of truth-light let forth into this world that it should have made a tremendous difference; and in a way, it did. But it's an uncanny feeling to have been present at Haight Street from when it was a nice Italian-American neighborhood, and to have seen what happened there. And here we are these few years down the line, and all these folks are saying,

"What happened?"

"Did anything happen?"

"No, nothing happened. If anything had happened, we'd notice."

Some dude with hair down the middle of his back saying,

"Naw, nothing happened. If anything had happened, we'd have noticed."

The President of the United States wears blue jeans and his old lady wears a tee-shirt that says, "Jimmy Buffet and the Coral Reefers." Male lawyers and stockbrokers at discos with **beauty-**

parlor hairdos and earrings say,

"No, no, nothing happened. There was no great cultural upheaval."

But it really did happen. It just really did happen. We just look back down it, and we see how twisted and how distorted in this short ten years—and then you have to look 2,500 years ago to Gautama Buddha, 2,000 years ago to Christ, 18,000 years ago to Lord Krishna, and look back on those occasions, understanding what happened to the message that came down in Haight Street— look back on those people and try to understand what they said to us two thousand, twenty-five hundred years ago, and how much of it comes through clear and undistorted, and how much of it means what we know it means.

Sometimes I feel like coming out like some mythological character and wasting all the superstitions. Various things pass through my mind, like,

"14.95 pyramid power: a piece of coat-hanger wire. How long can a Guatemalan peasant live on $14.95? How obscene is it to sell counterfeit religious relics home-made in your little factory out of fifteen cents worth of coathanger, and sell it for $14.95?"

How immoral is it to say,

"Enlighten your taste buds!" in an advertisement in a spiritual magazine?

Or ads for "change your luck" and "weird occult."

You have to see what the unmistakable message was. You have to look at that thing in Haight Street not in linear terms or Aristotelian terms, but in McLuhan terms. What was the message of that medium? Because there was a medium created there; we are talking in it now. Millions of people, all over the United States and all over the world, are tuned into and communicate with this medium we are talking in now. One that assumes healing and love and truth and God and telepathy. A medium was created.

I remember when the only people who believed in psychic energy were ninety year-old ladies with lavender dresses and pink Cadillacs. Nobody else in this country believed in it then. Everyone else thought those old ladies were quaint, and they were the only ones who had any juice at the time, but unmistakably there came through the power of love and the potency of the human being, the always-presence of God.

Folks are always coming along to turn me onto the latest thing, that if you just stand on your head for half an hour, count from four hundred and seventy-seven backwards, stick your tongue up your left nostril, you're going to achieve transcendence. I've been transcendant, off and on, for ten or eleven years . . . in the bathtub, on the outhouse . . . without sticking my tongue up my left nostril or any of the other patented ways that are advertised now.

I used to talk about Raja Yoga—the Yoga of Discrimination. It is so important to learn how to tell the difference between real Spirit and real life and real love, and superstitions, money scams, power gambles, spiritual and psychic chain letters. It's really necessary that we don't be superstitious, because we are dealing with the real stuff; and rather than being superstitious about the energy, you should be as careful and as hip as an electrician should be, because the energy is _like_ electricity: it doesn't have any value judgment on it, and it's dangerous if you don't know what to do with it. All the old books say, for instance, that you can't practice Kundalini Yoga if you don't have a teacher. The reason they say that is, if you practice Kundalini Yoga you're going to get some energy up, and when you get some energy up, you're going to illuminate your consciousness, and if your consciousness is full of a lot of selfishness and stupidity and garbage and stuff that has been laying about meaning to be swept out for years and you haven't done it, when that conciousness gets illuminated, you're going to wig—you'll nutty right out. That's why you're supposed to have a teacher for Kundalini Yoga: so you can have a relativity point around, who can say,

"Whoa, baby, down baby, easy, easy."

Talking to alcohol is hard, and talking to downers is hard, and talking to an entrenched superstition is _very_ hard. And there's an interesting thing about magic: if you be too negative, you don't get to do your magic at all. If you go around being negative, it's hard to do any magic in your presence; but the Spirit is afoot on the world and the petty magicians run around in the presence of the Spirit doing little magic, and the people across the world be so kind, so patient and so good, almost to a fault, as they say . . .

When all this started, my consciousness was reduced to zilch, zero, and I crawled back up many times, caught myself putting it back together wrong and kicked it down again, and didn't accept one until I found a direction of growth I felt I could live with, and rejected all of the *a priori* asssumptions of mankind, and put them back together as they were needed, which ones were needed, and we went through a lot of different changes.

In the greater background, you read *The Mother Earth News*, you read *Rolling Stone*, maybe do rock 'n' roll sometimes, know about some spiritual teachers, know several swamis and yogis, probably drunk a little Celestial Seasonings tea in your time. People arrive with that cultural thing on. Well, there was a kind of purity in that sheep dip we all got dipped in, and we want to maintain that purity.

All of the psychic press magazines, new age media, advertise and scratch each other's backs for circulation and money, and be dishonest in every way that the big publications taught them how to be. What is the difference between them and *Hustler*? They sell advertising that they don't believe in for money in a spiritual magazine; and spiritual means that you won't sell out, doesn't it? Doesn't it mean that you make your decisions out of your principles and not out of your pocket or your stomach? Some of our folks have been out to book fairs and food fairs, and have gotten to see the commercial thing that's happening—the New Age merchant on the hoof.

All of that is symbolic of the general entropy of our realization. I am trying to say that we have had a realization over the past ten or twelve years. We have had a realization. It is important that we protect our realization and don't let it run down. That leads one to a thorny problem. If one has seen miracles, and one sees falseness sold to people under the label of a miracle, one tends to want to say something. You feel like saying,

"Oh, man, I had some of the real kind once. That isn't it."

But you have to be careful about going around being negative about anything. What are you going to do? *You can eradicate superstition in your own life.*

Truth is the real key to eradicating superstition in yourself. When you're speaking truth, you're dealing with God. God is truth. And you're also dealing with love: God is love. God is beauty. And if you want to say something to someone, even though it's true, you should notice, Is it beautiful? Is it loving? Is it really expressing God as you want God expressed? A lot of people express a God that would scare the pants off them. It's not that. We need to speak a lot of truth, all the time.

I said once that there were people who weren't paying close enough attention to tell the difference between me and Sun Myung Moon. A shocking statement, perhaps.

I can show you my books about how I do my thing; but if you haven't done your homework, you can't even study my books. You cannot ask me if I'm honest—or you can, but what good is it going to do you? What would I say if I was honest? What would I say if I was dishonest?

Now, if you want to know if I'm just a really skillful poolshooter who has run down a great scam on all these people for the last ten years, the only way you can check it is to teach yourself to _go over the problems and the work for yourself,_ so you can work the problem for yourself and understand it—that's the only way you can know. That's the only way I ever learned anything I ever believed. In high school, they teach you the steps of the scientific method—it's simple—and you can check everything against that.

Superstition is an interesting thing, because we have a set of phenomena which, although undeniably real, so far are only able to be empirically verified by the human organism. I have felt love; I have felt telepathy; I've been hit by blasts of _stonedness_ that have knocked me down. And you have, too. But no needles have wiggled. There is not yet a _stonemeter._ It would be very simple if there was a stonemeter.

The hand is quicker than the eye. And in questions of psychic phenomena, I admit no second-party evidence. But one time, while I was banged on a psychedelic (which probably makes it so that nothing-I-say-really-means-anything-because-it's-all-subjective), the old lady of one of my friends, apparently, to what I could feel and see, cut my index finger off with a pair of scissors. And I felt the pain, an incredible burst of pain from my hand. I heard a sound like scissors cutting many layers of blanket—_Screee!_

I heard the scissors do that, and then she jumped up and ran away. I saw my hand there and that finger missing and a pool of blood on the floor. _And then I saw the pool of blood disappear, and I saw my finger materialize back into place._ Now, I'm not going to put it on you that that happened in the material plane. That's where I experienced it, but I'm not going to put it on you there.

In this kind of work, I really trust the vibrations. Sometimes I have to fall back on being purely subjective and say I just don't like the vibrations. There's a lot of stuff happening out there, and it sends out vibes that I can feel; and some of that stuff, the first vibe that hits you feels funny. How many hot teachers have we heard of that are supposed to be the coming, this time's instantaneous zap-them-all, nobody'll ever-have-to-get-stoned-on-dope-again, we're-all-going-to-fly-free-forever. And of all of those that we've heard about, think of the ones who have proved to be anything like their promo. Mother Teresa. Bucky Fuller.

I get a lot of spiritual junk mail sent to me, and the first thing I look for is the price. There's another team coming from India, an old guru and his young disciples coming to this country to straighten us all. They only charge twelve hundred and fifty dollars for a session. Children in arms, only fifteen dollars a week. Twenty-five dollars a week for older children, a hundred dollars a week for grownups. Very expensive brochure, good four-color printing job, in his pictures he has good microphones and good tape recorders, obviously all high quality expensive equipment. The whole thing takes place at a big kind of resort hotel that you have to rent the whole hotel to do it in. **This is symbolic of the generalized entropy of our realization.**

Nobody can tell me they're God. You can God in front of me and I'll be respectful, but don't tell me you're God. I get tired of hearing that old jive. I've heard it thousands of times from folks who wanted me to know that they alone, uniquely and individually, to the exclusion of everyone else, are God. In a pig's ear they are.

Solid Gold

This thing really kicked off ten, fifteen years ago, even longer ago than that. There was a great burst of spiritual energy that happened, and it gave birth to a tremendous number of teachers. Schools were just proliferating, there was so much juice. The knowledge of what went on was very plain. There used to be a San Francisco tripper who wrote continuity for the Marvel Comic *Doc Strange,* and he wrote stories about how somebody had pulled the forelock from this giant and released the power of magic that had been bottled for hundreds of years, like Pandora's Box. All of a sudden, hobbyist astrologers and hobbyist palmists and people like that suddenly started having power and energy all over the world. In the comic strip, Doc Strange was given twenty-four hours to get things together or they were going to have to put this planet off-limits.

And it's really like that, because there just wasn't much real information or real knowledge about Spirit, except in a very few places. When you talk about Tibet now, you can run down to your local head shop and pick up a Dorghe, or you can pick up a Yab/Yum cushion—they have a whole cultural thing there. It used to be that to get into Tibet and learn anything, people would have to disguise themselves as Sherpa bearers, like they take up Mount Everest; they'd have to carry big packs, and go sneak in on somebody's train of baggage. And if anybody found out that they were a gringo, they got kicked out of the country immediately. They didn't used to let them hang around: it was a Holy city. And now there are cars running around in the U.S. with plastic Tibetan stick-ons in their windows.

Some teachers are really out for the people, and teaching skills. Others are building empires, and there's a whole continuum in between. Various media are coming out lately, on debunking expeditions—there was a documentary on television, pre-empting the regular program, that was an hour-long presentation on Sun Myung Moon and on Scientology. It was pretty heavy, because they were really after them. A lot of it was just accurately reported stuff that I know to be true—since 1950, of my own experience. But some of it was stuff that showed that they were also not without their slant. For instance, they did subtle mind things. Sun Moon's interpreter was a colonel in Korean Intelligence, and they implied that American Intelligence was who started Moon's first center in this country. But whenever they showed the picture of Moon's interpreter, they'd make that little sound like on *Mission: Impossible!* of the slide projector going *Chuuk!* And every time they showed that dude's picture, they'd go *Chuuk!*—doing a little number on your head. The television can do numbers on your head while they're telling you about doing numbers on your head.

On the Farm, I said that we should be efficient enough and together enough that we could make it if we weren't tax-exempt. I was really serious, because that structure may change. People are thinking about changing that structure right now: people like Sun Moon and Hubbard have been abusing the non-profit church tax-exempt system so badly that the government is getting mad.

In Scientology, everybody tithes ten per cent to Hubbard, in the first place. Then they all buy treatments from each other, and Hubbard gets ten per cent of any transactions where people buy treatment from each other. You can start off with someone giving someone else a hundred dollars for auditing, and Hubbard gets ten dollars of that. Then the auditor wants to buy himself some auditing, so he buys ninety dolars of auditing, and Hubbard gets nine dollars of that; and the dude he bought it from can turn around and buy some more auditing from somebody else, and Hubbard gets eight dollars and ten cents of *that*. And the government is *hot*, because he's into twenty million dollars or so.

This documentary was national network, and preempted local programming: it was a federal piece of business. And they're just raising hell about Sun Myung Moon's tax-exempt status. They said,

"We're not even talking about his religious practice; we're talking about his being hooked up with South Korean Intelligence."

At the same time that kind of thing is going on, _Psychology Today_ runs an article entitled, "A Cool-Eyed Look at Commercial Mysticism." How's that for a title? They come on pretty strong, like that most of these outfits are peddling relaxation as enlightenment; and there's a certain point to what they're saying. There _is_ a difference between relaxation and enlightenment. But the main thing is that the psychologists and the television are the _de facto_ high priests of the culture, because there aren't any religious priests who have any juice. The psychologists and the television have lots of juice, and they are trying to do the same number they did when the scientific method first hit Europe hundreds of years ago—the Establishment ruled out the real magic and the real Holy Spirit and the real healing energy, along with all the bogus and bunko that goes on. The closest _Psychology Today_ came to admitting anything was real was their statement that _for there to be so many counterfeiters, there must be such a thing as gold_

I know magic and esoteric practices, some Hindu, Sanskrit, Tibetan, Shinto and whatnot, but most of my time is put into loving one another and getting along together, trying to make something like the Farm work. I'm not trying to make it work so we can have a place to live. It's nice for us to have a place to live, but that's not the important thing. The question is at hand on the earth, _whether anyone can get along well enough to be viable. Is there anybody getting along well enough just to exist here on this planet?_

This is the time when the world is breaking down in the way Marshall McLuhan predicted. He was really a prophet. He talked about how people were going to have different loyalties: it wasn't going to be all the same church any more, or speaking the same language. Different loyalties would be created by things like all listening to the same radio station. For a real example, there are military implications in the rise of terrorist and hijackers. These phenomena are the result of the breakdown of national boundaries, and along with that, a breakdown of their insulating abilities.

Jamaica didn't used to have to worry about us too much: Cuba was in between us and it was a long way down there. Now you just fly right over Cuba and land right on them.

There are people who are technicians at building people's loyalty: like politicians. What we're doing on the Farm is trying to create something so reasonable that it doesn't offend people. It should have, like a well-designed airplane, no drag. It can sail a long way. So it should be reasonable, easy-to-understand; it shouldn't insult your intelligence. And at the same time, it shouldn't sell out the reality of Holy Spirit.

I had a lot of confusion in the early days when I was learning stuff. Many of the people I hung out with were undeniably extremely telepathic, people who could move the energy and could make a meeting turn bright and white, people who knew how to run a communion, but who, at the same time, were obviously not changed enough to alter their lifestyle. I'd see these people with access to all this incredible ecclesiastical magic, and not be that cool.

When you see that kind of stuff, you can't just go and flash your piece of knowledge in somebody's face like a firecracker, and expect to blow their mind so bad they're going to change. What you maybe ought to do, rather than pop it in their face, is to hint at it. Don't even say it out loud, just hint at it.

There is the Christian idea of the Kingdom of Heaven, which implies two things. It implies a state of enlightenment, but it also implies a state of agreement among a bunch of people who see things that way. In the book of *Revelations,* it talks about the City of God, outside of which live sorcerers and all those that love a lie. And the City of God is also an agreement of the people. It is also a state, a *bardo,* or a *loka*. Those are technical terms in Tibetan for levels of consciousness that exist. There is a coherent set of laws that govern that set of consciousness; in fact, the laws are what you can recognize that set of consciousness by. And what they call the Kingdom of Heaven is a level of consciousness, a level of agreement.

The gesture of Jesus in Dali's painting of the Last Supper, where he has one finger pointing to the sky, is symbolic of that agreement: *I and my Father are One*. It's like he's saying Sangsara and Nirvana are One; there is no question of Heavens or Earths.

I have a picture of a Buddha whose belly is sucked in about four inches, and his ribs are all sticking out—he ain't one of your fat Buddhas, he has every rib sticking out, and the muscles in his neck are standing out; he is skinny and has a hard face. The title of this sculpture is _The Buddha in Hard Search._ I really like that picture.

Buddhist psychology says there is a state called Nirvana, which is beyond all states, beyond desire and all hankerings and cravings. Most people think you have to be dead to be there.

Everything in creation is One. All parts, whether of material nature or planes in between, all varieties and natures of reality, and all questions of realities as yet unthought of, are still all One, one phenomenon. And there is a certain amount of illusion that is possible in the human mind. In fact, there is a tremendous amount of illusion possible in the human mind. You can even put on a whole different movie than the one that is there.

I read a science fiction book in which a dude went to the government office to complain that he suspected the government was doping the people to keep them happy in hard times. He told the government official he suspected this was happening, and cited his evidence, and the official said,

"You don't even want to know what it's really like."

"What do you mean?"

The executive produces this powerful downer which, when you take a sniff, allows you to see the room as it really is—which is bare concrete walls and a dirt floor, and a two-by-four table that they're sitting at with a candle. They _had_ been in a marble-walled government office with marble steps, which was what he'd seen before he took a whiff of that stuff and looked around.

Then the official said,

"The illusion is even worse than you thought. You know all those new cars people are so happy about? Take a look out the window." And the people are walking down the street with their hands out in front of them, as if they were holding steering wheels.

The illusion is pretty thick in that tale, the sangsara is pretty heavy. Nirvana is supposed to be a _place of no illusion._

As a point of interest, that particular fiction tale was written by a writer I have recently discovered named Stanislaw Lem, who is one of the best-selling science fiction writers in the world, just now being noticed in the United States. He talks about illusion and *sangsara* all through those places. What would you rather know? Would you rather be in a comfortable illusion, or would you rather be in kind of a rough place that was really where it was at?

In another scene in that book, the guy is running away from the baddies, and he ends up hiding in the sewer. He goes on these long imagined head trips that take you down through all kinds of weird places, which he gets back from by thrashing around down in the sewer until he falls off the thing he was on, and plunges down into the sewer. And when he comes up, coughing and gagging, he's grateful for the reality. Lem has a nice head.

But if you're a Bodhisattva, there is no hurry, and no place to go, because you are where you want to be, by your own choice. And if you don't have any illusions, wherever you are is Nirvana. Or sangsara, depending on where you're at: Nirvana and Sangsara are One. You almost have to read Sanskrit footnotes to get any more juice out of that.

There is an interesting phenomenon that arises out of that psychedelic state of consciousness, known as *imprinting*. The early experiments on imprinting were done on ducks. When a mother hatches out her baby ducks, they all imprint on her as mother. When she walks, they walk. It's a familiar sight, the duck family moving—Mama duck followed by all the little babies strung out behind her in a row, following her everywhere she goes: they don't get lost. One time, intentionally or not, when they hatched out a lot of ducks for some experiments, the ducks became hooked on this lab assistant instead of their mother, and the ducks would follow this lab assistant everywhere. He was the one that fed them, and he was the one that was with them when they were hatched. They just imprinted on this lab assistant, just called him "Mommy," and that was it, and followed him around. They have some other baby ducks that are kind of neurotic: just to see if they'd imprint on anything that was around, they had some baby ducks imprint on a basketball.

When you are born, and first come into the world, you imprint. When you wake up in the morning after a night's sleep, you imprint. When you have a psychedelic trip, you imprint. If you have an epileptic seizure or an anemia blackout, when you come back, you re-enter. You imprint, and you have to be careful what you imprint on.

People have come to me who have tripped in a rock hall and come home with a specific piece of lyrics imprinted in their mind that made them neurotic for months, because they took something personal out of the lyrics and assumed that it was about them, and become obsessive/compulsive about it for months, from imprinting on a random piece of rock 'n' roll—you go in with a sensitive, open, psychedelic condition if you get off at all, and from there what's in front of you should be pure and clean, because you want to soak it up.

This whole thing about imprint is really heavy, because you can imprint in ways that last your whole life. There's a whole field of discovery in medicine called _bonding_, which is an imprint phenomenon. Marshall Klaus is a pediatrician at Case Western Reserve who is doing studies on maternal-infant bonding. He looked at situations where the babies were taken away from the mothers and not given back to them for a day or two, compared to the ladies who were given the child immediately upon birth and allowed uninterrupted contact except for being cleaned up once in a while. The ladies that don't have their children with them at this early stage show a statistically higher history of child abuse. His studies show that ladies who don't get to have their child with them right away tend to be uncompassionate with their children, and abuse them to a higher extent than the ladies who get their kids right away.

Imprinting is an instinctual act, and the instinctive part of it is to imprint at all. What you imprint on is variable. That's exactly the point: the reason ducks can imprint on a laboratory assistant or a basketball is because they are doing it instinctively. It's not a reasoned act or anything, it's just the highest survival thing the baby can do. Anything that you see with an instinctual response like that is usually a survival mechanism: they're pre-programmed to imprint on the first thing they run into, which is usually the mother duck, over a long period of history. They don't usually have some mad scientist doctor messing around.

Imprinting unconsciously conditions your behavior. In fact, most people you meet on the street are a clutter of imprints walking around, thinking that they are somebody.

That's what we're trying to do, is to get above that clutter of imprints. That's why I put such tremendous value in psychedelic states of mind, because you can rise above all conditionings and see them. You can look clear into your subconscious and see conditioning, and make a decision to not do that anymore, and become unconditioned.

I recommend that people meditate at least once a week, perhaps more often than that, because part of what you do when you meditate is get quiet long enough to see if you have any heavy conditionings or imprinting on you that you're all obsessive/compulsive about, and can't let go of. These are things you would never notice if you never got quiet, so you have to be quiet now and then and listen to what's really going on in there, and find out if your reaction to something comes from a piece of conditioned behavior.

Most folks are completely conditioned. Gurdjieff sounds so cynical when he talks about how everybody is conditioned, that everybody is asleep except for a very few who are awake for one reason or another. Folks are not always asleep just because they were raised by some fat, dumb culture that conditioned them negative-life-force. There are also people from a culture that is so poor that they never have time to be anything other than hungry.

We are running a higher level of mind technology than the greater culture. We take it for granted that you can be something without being angry or powerful, that you can do something about it. *That assumption itself is just solid gold.* It hardly exists anywhere in the world, except among places like this. There are a lot of places like this; they just aren't the noisiest ones. Fortunately, it's not a question of who's the most popular or who has the most money.

Gurdjieff said there's a certain amount of consciousness in the world, and some folks get a lot of it and others get less, as if there was a limited amount. Well, Gurdjieff's a bit of an elitist. Holy Spirit is not bound by who is present or anything. There is an infinite amount of Holy Spirit. God is infinite.

If you want to push consciousness on people, where you say this person is a preemie, or this person is enlightened, or this person is a pre-Clear and that person is a Clear, or that kind of thing, you might get yourself into a finite number of titles you can hand out; but if you are just willing to let knowledge flow forth like a fountain, and let people have it like they want, and don't make them have to have Ph.D.'s or anything after their name to symbolize that they have touched the knowledge—if you just see that everyone is doing their best, and if those folks who have trouble stretching can hang tight with the majority, they will be carried and they will be stretched. Some people talk in terms of winners and losers, but what we are saying is that

We are all going to do it together,

and that

Consciousness is not an individual thing. It may require an active choice not to be an elitist. But it's the answer to the riddle. It's a mistake to think that the riddle is just a riddle. You don't really want to get off the wheel—everybody that gets there comes back.

We are only immune to imprinting if we are actively paying attention. Somebody asked Krishnamurti if he dreamed very much.

"Not very much," he replied. "I pay attention the first time it comes in."

Now, if you're not immune to imprinting, shouldn't you identify with the highest symbol you can? But you don't want to identify with a symbol, because a symbol ain't real. Two bits and a Congressional Medal of Honor will get you on a streetcar. But God is real, and if you identify with God, truly you are immortal. If you identify with a symbol, you're liable to find yourself having to make distinctions that you shouldn't have to make. But if you're talking about the Christ Spirit as it appears in the Universe, under whatever alias it may appear under, that's obviously where it's at.

And it's important to put in the clause about "under all aliases." It disturbs people whose idea of a savior is someone who doesn't wear any armor, dresses very simply and is obviously very vulnerable, when they see a culture like Mexico, where that consciousness is represented by a feathered rattlesnake. They don't worship a feathered rattlesnake, they worship *that consciousness,* as it appears in Quetzalcoatl, the feathered serpent.

It may get translated into weird kinds of languages, but, man, those are real people. You could take someone from five thousand years ago in the ancient Mayan places down there with all strange languages that you never heard of, and run him through enough communication that you could talk with him just like you talk with me or the person next to you.

They proved that during World War II, when they landed in places like New Guinea in Africa, where there were Stone Age people. They found some people who were at that kind of level, and apprenticed them as airplane mechanics. The Seabees came in and threw down a bunch of metal netting and a bunch of airplanes come flying in, and we start hiring the natives and hooking them up working at the airfields, and in a matter of months you have people from the Stone Age working in the Jet Age. Why not?

So it works not just from country to country, but it works in time, too. You could pull out a Roman Centurion and teach him to tune an Oldsmobile, or build a church.

So we're all really the same folks, all over this rock, and we have to leave our definitions open enough that we don't accidentally exclude anybody, because Lord knows we don't want to exclude anybody.

No Dust, No Mirror, No Mind

I want to tell you just a little bit about the Sixth Patriarch, because there's something in his story that's relevant to something else I want to talk about.

There was this fellow down in China. He couldn't read or write or anything like that, because those were really high arts in those times, and he was a simple woodcutter. He was going along into town one day, probably to sell a load of wood, and he came past a street corner where somebody was speaking a certain kind of talk which he heard as he went by, and it stopped him in his tracks. He went back to where this man was standing and said,

"What is that stuff? What are you saying? What kind of talking is that? That's the first thing I ever heard that made such good, clean sense. That's some very good stuff, what is that stuff? Where do I find out more about that stuff?"

And the monk said that was part of the *Diamond Sutra*, the teaching of Buddha, and if you wanted to know more about that teaching, you could go out to the monastery.

Now he was un-hip to learning or religion or anything like that, so he went out to the monastery to check it out. When he got there, there was a funny sort of thing going on. The teacher was getting ready to take a successor. He felt he was getting old, and he was ready to give transmission of Mind and of the Dharma, that is, to take a successor, along the lines of Christianity taking a new Pope, somebody to follow the old line. A lot of people thought the teacher's meditation master, who worked for him and ran the meditation in the monastery, was probably going to be the man.

They had a contest about who would write a poem to express the realization of the Dharma. The meditation master wrote a poem which said,

Our body is the Bodhi-tree,
And our mind a mirror bright.
Carefully we wipe them hour by hour
And let no dust alight.

That was designed to express his realization and his learning. The woodcutter came through, walking down the hallway, and heard someone reading that poem up on the wall, and thought,

"That ain't quite right. That ain't exactly it."

And he had somebody write down his poem:

There is no Bodhi-tree
Nor stand of a mirror bright.
Since all is void,
Where can dust alight?

And all these thousand monks of the monastery said,

"Wow! How about that?"

And the old teacher came through and saw this happening and thought,

"This is sort of a dangerous situation." He went over and erased the "No dust, no mirror, no Mind," as if it didn't mean much, and said,

"Oh. I see I have a new monk here."

To the woodcutter, he said,

"Go down and work in the stables."

The woodcutter did what he was told, and went down and worked in the stables. Later, he worked pounding the rice. One night, as he was pounding the rice, the old teacher came down to him and said,

"Is the rice ready?"

"It's *been* ready," said the woodcutter.

And the Fifth Patriarch signalled for him to come up and meet him in the middle of the night. When he asked if the rice was ready, he meant,

"So you really know where it's at, huh?"

And when the woodcutter answered that the rice was ready, he meant,

"You bet."

They all lived in a big barracks, and the woodcutter came to the teacher's room, and they threw a robe over themselves, which happened to be the cloak of old Bodhidharma, who was described as the broken-toothed old Hindu who brought Buddhism to China. The teacher told him a few truths and they sat together under this cloak, head to head, talking about it quietly, and one thing hit him really hard, and he said,

"Who could have thought that the Essence of Mind is intrinsically pure!

"Who would have thought that the Essence of Mind is intrinsically free from becoming or annihilation!

"Who would have thought that all things are the manifestation of the Essence of Mind!

"Who could have imagined it would be like that?" and he really liked it a lot.

Then the old teacher gave him a robe and a bowl.

"You take this robe, which is the robe of Bodhidharma; and take this bowl, which is His begging bowl; but don't pass them on any more. I'm going to pass them on to you because I want you to have a solid symbol that you've received the transmission; but don't make a fetish out of it. Let it go and don't use it for the transmission any more. But what you have to do now is split, because there's a thousand mad monks in this monastery. You'd better haul, baby."

So he took the cloak and the bowl and he hauled. He got to the top of the hill and looked down and saw two hundred men chasing him, coming down through the valley, and he kept on hauling; later on, one of them caught up with him, and he said,

"I can't take this."

He set down the cloak and bowl and said,

"Take them. Just take them. Don't bug me."

The fellow went over to grab them, and couldn't lift them off the ground. He tried, and he strained, and he pulled, but he couldn't lift them off the ground. Finally, he said,

"Look. This isn't even what I want. I want what you _really_ got. I don't want the old bowl and robe, anyway."

I guess that was his first student.

The woodcutter stayed in the woods for about fifteen years, until he thought things had blown over and it was cool again. He began walking, and he drifted down to the capital. He came in and sat down, and there was a bunch of heavy monks sitting around talking about it, and he joined the conversation. Immediately, they all said,

"Who? What? Just listen to him!"

They asked him a few more questions and it kept getting heavier. The more questions they asked him, the better he knew the answers. He kept answering them and answering them, and finally they asked him who he was. He said he was the Sixth Patriarch, and they believed him. He hung out there, and they went down in the basement in the old cathedral and dug out dusty, dusty old books written centuries before by very heavy Holy men, and they brought them upstairs and they read them to him, because he couldn't read. They read the old books to him, and he told them what they meant.

The place about no dust, no mirror and no Mind is another way of saying that the One Mind is made up of non-synchronous thought. There's One Mind that is *the* Mind; and at the same time, just as truly, there is No Mind.

But there is an amazing amount of superstition present in the New Age. Astrology, numerology, the *I Ching*, Tarot. The only objective significance to the number seven is that it seems to be a natural part of the octave scale—seven and a repeat make eight, which is your octave. And lots of stuff runs in octaves. A lot of stuff also runs in triads and fifths. But numerology is related to the ways that vibrations mesh and intermingle and stuff like that. These things are like pinball machines, because you get in there and you do all these operations with all these numbers. What you're really doing when you're doing those numbers, casting those yarrow stalks, dealing those cards, is giving your mind some bubble gum to work on while you retire back with your soul and find out what's happening.

There's also pyramidology, of which there are two schools currently rampant—the square base school, and the triangle base school. One of them, as far as I can tell, is completely without merit; and the other one looks to me to be pretty well where it's at. The first one, we could call King Tut's school, which is the one that comes out of the magical properties of the grave of King Khufu and stuff like that. It's pretty much a shuck, and it's a shame to see a lot of otherwise bright people fall into such Mickey Mouse things.

The other school of pyramidology is Mr. Buckminster Fuller's, in which he points out that the triangle is the natural building block of the universe. It's in cellular relationships, crystalline relationships, atomic relationships, mathematical relationships, geometrical relationships—it's the basic building block of this whole thing, and it was only due to accidents of culture that we ended up with the system we have, which is so _square_.

I believe that demonology is superstitious. I'd rather have my own hallucinations. I mean, I see some things that would scare you back up your tree. One of the good things Tim Leary said before he disappeared back into the _sangsara_ was that, if you looked at the old Tibetan books where they had people being rent by terrible monsters and griffins and dragons, that the modern trippers who wandered into those same territories were more likely to find themselves accosted by giant unfeeling, inhuman science fiction-y machines and robots; and there is indeed a territory where it's like that; but you're the one who puts clothes on your monsters.

The superstition is that anybody who can manifest up a little juice is a guru. But it's more a question of folks' astral mobility, their outfront ability to whomp a little magic on you once in a while. It bears no relationship to their spiritual coolness or integrity or purity, for there is a category we are told of called _magicians_; and a magician can magish, or he isn't worthy of his name.

I know a dude who can do an out-front piece of magic, who has since retired from the Holy Man business and considers himself not to be doing that any more. But I saw him do out-front magic before my very eyes. When the Ashoke Fakir was at one of the first Holy Man Jams in San Francisco, he was leading the kind of a chant where he got the energy flowing back and forth across the room until at a certain point of his chant it was flowing back and forth so obviously that everybody could see that the energy was manifest, flowing back and forth on the wings of this chant that the Ashoke was doing with them. At a certain point, one of the Shoke's students, who was just an incorrigible rip-off, decided that he was going to catch this here juice on the bounce and take it. So the juice went back and it hit the back of the auditorium, came flowing back toward the stage like a great big tidal wave, and this friend of mine leaped up from sitting behind the Shoke, screaming _Yaaaahhhhh!_

As all the juice was coming down toward him and while he was still up in the air, the Shoke left the ground and jumped higher and screamed louder and hit back on the stage with his arms extended and an eight-inch purple glow around him, and just stood there with this glow on, and everybody applauded and the glow gradually faded away—because his bucket was a little leaky. He could magish. He had a craft, and he could do his number. He could do something, and I hope he hasn't forgotten that he knew how to manifest energy once.

There are basically two ways of looking at things like the Tarot. One of them is as an esoteric book of knowledge; and the other is as an oracle of divination. As an oracle of divination, I'd prefer reading old Kleenexes. You can tell things from old Kleenexes, like is it yellow or is it green could be viral or bacterial—there's a certain amount of information in them—but if you use the Tarot as an oracle of divination, that's another one of those robot pinball machines which, plus a little paranoia, could buy you a ticket off the Golden Gate Bridge.

As an esoteric book of knowledge, the Tarot is a symbol system, and you can read and study in this symbol system and it's just like studying yoga or something, once you get past the superstition. It has a crust around it like the rind of a canteloupe, and inside that you're just talking about character and personality, which was all done in metaphors in those days because the Church was so heavy on you that everybody was afraid to say it out loud—so astrology and all those were ways of keeping the knowledge alive, putting it in code. Even palmistry leads to yoga somewhere.

In fact, that's just the justification people give for most of those trips: they say,

"Oh, you can't say *this* is a strange trip; if you push this trip a little farther, you get yoga."

You can take yoga right off the top if you want, or magic or love. Alchemy is another one of those disciplines. Schools like that are said to have an outside layer, a middle layer, and an inside layer—exoteric-mesoteric-esoteric. In the outside layer, people don't know what's happening much. In the middle layer are a bunch of people trying to get hip. In the inside layer are a bunch of folks who have a pretty good idea of what's happening. And that's the secret of it. It's not that somebody who's running a school says,

"Okay, this is the esoteric classroom over here, . . ."

It just automatically arranges itself that way.

In alchemy, they talk about finding the Philosopher's Stone, with which you can transmute dross, ordinary old stuff, into gold. There are all these various metals that you're going to melt together and do all these fancy configurations with; and the names of all the metals and flowers are of astrological significance: they are about certain mind states. The aspect of Mercury, for instance, is supposed to be a very fast, bright, intelligent, amusing and witty conciousness. So when you get into alchemy, it's not even about taking lead and making it into gold. The Philosopher's Stone is true knowledge. You touch it to you, which is ordinary stuff, yourself, and it changes you and your life and your experience. Realization and understanding is what they're talking about, but they have to couch it in these weird codes with seven layers to them. That code doesn't seem too serious a code to us right now, perhaps; but during the Middle Ages, when there weren't that many who could read anyway, it kept a lot of folks out of it while still, in a way, preserving some knowledge.

That's what the Masons and the Rosicrucians and all those folks figure they're doing, is trying to preserve esoteric knowledge. They think that the esoteric knowledge can be preserved in the books and the words—but the esoteric knowledge can only be preserved in the heart of someone who is alive, who's _stoned_. I mean _stoned_ in its generic sense, for those folks who will write me letters later on.

A Holy Monument

Sometimes I think of the Farm as a Holy monument. I used to think Holy monuments were just statuary art; but I begin to understand it more. A Holy monument really means that *something happened to you that you thought was important enough that you built that monument*, and maybe months and years down the line when you've forgotten a lot of it, you can go back and look at that big old stone thing and say,

"Why'd I do that? I must have felt really strongly about it. If I don't remember exactly why I did that real good, maybe I should investigate. It was heavy to me once; shouldn't it be heavy to me still? If it ain't heavy to me, it's just because I'm forgetting."

Man is in a strange situation. On the one side, there's the danger of becoming so jaded, so sophisticated, so blase that nothing mystifies you or makes you wonder or blows your mind or gets you off any more; and on the other side there is the possibility of forgetting there are Holy things.

One of the things that can cause you to forget is your ego. Your ego is just your identity. There's no value judgment on it one way or the other, any more than there's a value judgment on electricity or microscopes or anything like that; it's just your viewpoint. Without your viewpoint, you don't have one. People without stable viewpoints used to be called innocents. And the only reason it's a hassle is that it's such a fine and fancy camera that quite a few of us fall to playing with the camera, instead of taking pictures.

"Wow! Dig the rangefinder! Wow! Dig that depth-of-field!"

Your ego isn't your personal self; that's why it's so funny to be on a trip about it, because it ain't even yours. There is a teaching which says that God is the sense of I-ness, wherever it appears in the Universe. That's a sub-definition, under the All, the Totality, of course. But that's the magic of it—the relationship between the Totality and the individual. Each of us is like a little corner off a holograph film. It contains the Totality, and maybe the resolution isn't that fine and it's a little small, but it contains the Totality. Each one of us contains the totality, and that's a miracle. Here we sit inside here, very mortal—a semi-hard jelly, you can poke a hole in us with a sharp stick, we're not really very heavy stuff on this end, vulnerable to mosquitoes, lightning, rattlers, staph, herpes, *vulnerable*—and on the other end, we contain this whole manifestation. And we *are* the lightning.

I ran across something of Gary Snyder the other day, and I really liked it. In one of his most recent statements, they were questioning him about sitting ten-hour *sesshins* and he said,

"The only time I ever sat a ten-hour *sesshin* was when I was in the monastery and was forced to; other than that, I wouldn't do it, because somebody has to get the tomatoes in."

Snyder said that if you're going to set up for a lifetime of ten-hour *sesshin*, you're setting up for a lifetime of somebody else supporting you; and we're not in a position where a quarter of us can go off to a monastery and be supported by the rest of us so they can sit ten-hour *sesshins*. Everybody ought to meditate for themselves. He recommends an hour a day. But he says we ought to get used to the idea that we're not going to have those long-time *sesshins* very much, and what we have to do is *learn to make the work we do be our meditation*. I hadn't heard from him in years. It was good to hear him talking like that.

This country's spiritual consciousness is still playing with the camera a lot. We need to develop those pictures and see what they were pictures of—like lots of hungry people, for instance, or species vanishing from the earth. Then we can acquire some real respect for the Holy.

We try to keep the land sacred. It's good stuff, and there have been people walking around here as long as we know about. We turn up arrowheads in the fields all the time, arrowheads and spearheads out of the creeks. This is good territory; people lived here. And we have it because we are the descendants of the conquerors. We're not really any different from the people with European names who run Guatemala—except insofar as we free-will choose to opt out of being that.

I had a nice guy who had a very good insight about a lot of things come on to me and say,

"Don't you think it limits your thing to have long hair and be hippies?"

I thought he'd missed an important ingredient about it. Before we get down to what are the *real* effects of messing around in Spirit and psychedelics and all, I'd have to say one of its weirdest and strongest effects is in transforming gringos into third-worlders. And about the only thing you can distinguish us by as a third-worlder is our hair. I really like it. In fact, to find hair like this and evidences of work at the same time, is almost miraculous.

Our hair is a Holy symbol. When we stood in the penitentiary and saw the good ol' boys come through with their big old greasy pompadours and get a little trim around the ears, and we came through and they took us down to the scalp and left us looking funny, we knew something was going on. Then we found out that the goon squad was waiting for us, all primed in the next room, because they figured we were not going to let them cut our hair; and if we'd argued a speck, they were ready to come and drag us out and throw us in solitary, where we could stay until we submitted to haircuts. It was plain that they thought it was really important, a really big deal to them. And it faked them out and judoed them a little bit when we just went along and let them cut it. We didn't particularly want to be marked in the pen, either. So just as well have short hair there. But they only cut it once. We got through with one haircut. We kept it tucked behind our ears until we got to a place where we could let it go. Had to smuggle it out. Many people have found fairly extreme temptations, like real good jobs and full scholarships and all kinds of stuff like that, dangled in front of them if they would just cut their hair.

Hair is like psychic antenna, and has objective purposes. It has a length that it comes to, like a horse's mane. They say a hair follicle puts out a six-year hair, and the length of your hair is what you can do in six years—the average length when you come to it. More for some people than for others.

Short hair is basically a European style, and one of the things about going to Europe that really wigged me was I only saw about fifty wild trees all the time I was in Europe. They're all trimmed into cubes and squares and archways and have their tops cut off flat, and they're trimmed down to little knobs and stuff—manicured back like a dog's tail or ears, when they cut them to make them hang different. All that kind of stopping-it-from-letting-it-get-out, and not-letting-you-find-out-what-it's-like-when-it's-out is very repressive; and a short haircut, if you look through historically, is a sign of a repressive society.

There were the roundheads and the cavaliers. The cavaliers were the creative, artistic—and also the royalty at the time. In those days it was a different trip. Now the roundheads are the royalty, and they have the government. There's no particular reason for people to be trimmed back this way.

The only reason that northern European, basically German and English cut, has become so prevalent across the world, is that it was exported into other countries along with money, trade, exploitation, colonialism, and stuff like that. That's the only reason that haircut was exported anywhere in the world. Nowhere else in the world did people wear that kind of hair. Monks shaved their head; other people grew their hair, pretty much. And that's the thing—it doesn't fit good under all those cookie-cutters. They stick a cookie cutter down on top of you and everything that sticks outside the cookie cutter is not acceptable. You can take a couple of people of grossly dissimilar looks, who are really different, and cut them back to short haircuts like that, and you can't tell them apart. You can have a couple of dark-haired dudes with a short haircut and let them grow out, and one of them has long, flowing, wavy curls, and the other has a big bush of a natural. But you can't tell when it's cut back, because that's what it's for, it's the uniformity. It ain't the sanitation. We have soap these days so strong the *government* thinks it's too strong.

We like to let our hair grow the way it naturally grows, without messing with it too much. It helps avoid vanity. There's an old Zen story about a master who became famous for repeatedly decking a lady student. Her problem was that she was so beautiful that every Zen master she went to fell in love with her, and couldn't tell her anything. So she got a little uppity about her looks with this one, and he just slugged her. She stayed with him for a long time.

The greater culture is really changing. The generation that got its mind blown is growing up, and taking responsibility and

becoming in charge of more things; and there are more and more
new opportunities opening up all the time. I've had the experience
of hitting on old Monday Night Class-ers in strange places behind
desks who say,

"I used to go to Monday Night Class. May I fix you up?"

There are a lot of folks out there who haven't seen me since
then who would fix me up if they had a chance. It's like that for all
of us.

If we laid back and dropped our standards, it would be hard on
us. There are a lot of people dedicated to keeping the standards up.
Each person should feel that they would try to do it if they were
the only one who still remembered, and they'd try to remind the
rest. That's how it has to come from each one of us. Like a
monument.

Some people rely on spiritual books to remember. But what
people say and what people mean is hard to get down to the real
nitty-gritty. I hardly believe in any miracles except the ones I see.
I've seen enough of them; it makes me tend to know and
understand there's plenty of other ones; these are not unique. But
there a bunch of people, especially in the United States, who are
hung up on specific phenomena they've read about in books.
These are otherwise quite nice and acceptable people, who would
be functional and capable of helping out in the world, except that
they're running around trying to hit on one specific phenomenon
some book told them was the one they had to have before they
were cool. That's the danger about that kind of book.

On the other hand, there is some very good stuff in books. Like
Gandhi in what he refers to as "Experiments in Truth." He'll curl
your hair, he cuts it so fine. He must have been doing his
homework for years and years to even be able to _see_ it as fine as he
cuts it. He amazes me where he gets down to about what's fair.
Uncompromising about it; just austere in his respect for truth.

You can learn that kind of thing from books. In _Autobiography of a
Yogi,_ there were several miracles of various kinds. I've seen other
ones—some similar ones and some different ones, and I haven't
seen all of those that are mentioned there—but what I really got
out of that book was the power of love between Yogananda and
Yukteswar, which is what that book is really about. They really
made an agreement. Yukteswar said,

"I'll give you all my ashrams, and if you ever see me falling out of God-consciousness, just lay your head in my lap and hip me, tell me about it; don't let me ever slide."

They made that strong agreement, and that's a heavy thing.

But you have to be careful about being hung up in specific miracles. It's like it says in the *Bible:*

"Everybody has different talents, but not all will have the same talents," and it mentions some of them. And people think that because the *Bible* mentions talking in tongues and two or three other talents, that that's the catalog. It's not at all.

The mind is capable of manifesting its electricity in as many different ways as the material plane can manifest *its* electricity. You have stuff in your mind that acts like television, radio, and radar, and all that other stuff that happens with macrocosmic electricity—all those different varieties and modes of communication are available to Mind—which are all miraculous. We're all telepathic. Folks get stoned and raise the Holy Spirit. I think that's the one.

"Where two or three are gathered in My name, I am there." It comes to a minimum-sized group.

On the other hand, there is a considerable amount of superstition going around. I think that rationalization, among other things, is one of the causes of superstition, because all that rationalization throws so much leak and slop into the system that it's hard to tell accurately what went on. That causes you to have a spacey view of what's going on, and your spacey view of what's going on would have a tropism, just like sodium and chloride do in atomic chemistry—a spacey head like that would have a tropism to fill up with wish-fulfillment.

A lot of superstition is wishful thinking, of wanting it to be that way, claiming it's that way. I've been told that every Presidential candidate since I started turning on smoked reefer himself and was going to legalize it when he was elected. I've been told that about all of them. Right-wingers, left-wingers, Nazis, whatnot. And it's because there's always somebody who will pass on a piece of word like that.

It's like what happened to Apple: when the word got out about Apple, that the Beatles' recording company would help out folks, it hit the old superstition machine and became invincible. And

Apple got hit on so many times that they got paranoid and quit doing it.

That's one of the things about living in a community: If you be paranoid, it's going to fixate on your friends and closest folks to you, because that's the nature of it. And hopefully they're the ones who love you and care for you enough to be able to say,

"No," and have enough sense to not be threatening and to let you off the hook.

When I say,

"You have to work it out," some people say it's constant encounter—but that's a groove, too, because on the other hand we live here pretty peacefully. There's not very much bad-hearted stuff; it's pretty safe for a kid to go around the Farm.

Saint Benedict understood something about community in his description of how to run a monastery:

"If any pilgrim monk come from distant parts and with wish as a guest to dwell in the monastery and will be content with the customs which he finds in the place, and do not perchance by his lavishness disturb the monastery; but is simply content with what he finds, he shall be received for so long a time as he desires. If, indeed, he find fault with anything or expose it reasonably and with the humility of charity, the Abbot shall discuss it prudently, lest perchance God had sent him for this very thing. But if he has been found gossipy and contentious in time of his sojourn as guest, not only ought he not be joined to the body of the monastery, but also it shall be said to him honestly that he must depart; and if he does not go, let two stout monks, in the name of God, explain the matter to him.

That is Saint Benedict, and that's how come there are Benedictines still.

Guarding Your Gourd

There is some information that people really need to know these days. It's about programming, enlightenment, deprogramming, copping, head-copping, bounty-hunting, religious practice, and brain-washing.

Some people think we have a random sort of a discipline, and they say,

"Where's the rules?"

In the Marine Corps, they used to call them the rocks and shoals, The Universal Code of Justice, and that's what folks tell me:

"Where's the rocks and shoals?"

It ain't that I'm holding back, and it ain't that I don't understand how to put up one of those—Hatha Yoga from 5:30 to 6:30, breakfast from 6:30 to 7:00, two hours meditation from here to there, and various sadhanas, then Jaya Yoga, Laya Yoga, Japa Yoga, Mantra Yoga, Yantra Yoga, and all of that jive.

Now there's a real problem right in there, because the idea is that you're going to change your consciousness. That's what folks are doing all this for; that's why anybody comes to see me, or any other teacher at all, is because they want to change their consciousness—and if you want to change your consciousness, there's a bunch of stuff that you have to do, one way or another.

For example, you make some kind of a break, not just symbolic, but some kind of a real break with your old life. Carlos Castaneda gives instructions. He says you don't tell anybody your right name, where you were born, nothing about you, so they can't get any handles on you, and so they have to deal with you on a purely psychic level, because they know nothing about you. He will not give you the magic of knowing his true name. That's kind of magicky, and people think it's kind of weird when they hear about that, but there's something understandable in there, because it's that break with the old life.

Then there's the kind of break with the old life that the folks they call the Jesus Freaks did. Those folks took, among other teachings from the *Bible,* the lines of Jesus where he said,

"I come to set brother against brother, father against son; and bring not peace, but a fiery sword. And he who will not leave his parents to follow me is not worthy of me."

Now that had been let lay for a few hundred years. Nobody had messed with that teaching for a long time; and when a group of folks came through and tried to activate that particular teaching, it outraged all of Christendom. But it was about the break with the old life, stated really powerfully, frighteningly to some folks.

I've seen that, and in some ways, I even understand it. All that really means, I think, is that you have to make choices for Life Force, and for Truth and what's right to the best of your ability; and if it causes you to have to change friends in order to be good, well, that's just the way it goes.

And then you have the style of Vedanta that's being taught in the United States by Bhaktivedanta's Hare Krishna people. Their way of making that break is to change your culture and let go of the name your folks gave you, and you assume a new Hindu name. And you change the way you look: you shave your head a different way, you give up the kinds of clothes you were raised with and have a new different kind of clothes—trying to make that break.

Another facet of consciousness is the idea that you're trying to remember your realization, or trying to attain realization. The way they do that particular yoga is to try to do something that uses up all your senses, in such a way that your mind stays free and you aren't distracted by outside things while you try to maintain a God-conciousness in your mind. Now that doesn't sound like too funny an idea to people who have been studying consciousness for years; but if you were somebody's mother, and they ran off to join some commune, and you heard about how they have them sit in rows, and they have them chant stuff in foreign languages, and they're supposed to listen to the chant so they can't hear anything but the chant go on, and then they have this little bag that they put their hand in, and they have their beads in there and they mess with the beads to keep their sense of touch occupied, and your whole family back at home hears that and says,

"Whoa! It sounds like they're getting their gourds, doesn't it?"

It does sound like somebody is copping their heads or something. But if you want to follow that Yoga and do that discipline, what do you do?

I teach that kind of thing differently. Rather than chant a mantra and run a little set of beads through your hand, you could learn to listen and write Morse Code. I've always thought it was far out that White Lightning could listen to you and converse with you and listen to Morse Code and write it down, all at the same time. I thought that was as good as some of the stuff they talk about Satchidananda can do. It is a discipline that does the same thing as the little bag of beads, but it's harder to do, actually. What we are trying to do is take our yogas out of your real life, not to manufacture things to use up our senses with when we have this _humongous_ amount of work to do—which would use up all of our senses, all of our muscles, all of our intelligence and all of our courage for as long as any of us cared to plow it into it, and will if we're lucky. And it's supposed to do that thing for our consciousness.

But I am not going to say that that classic old method that has been passed down for five thousand years is bad. I can't do that. I'd love to study more of it, even. I read the old books; my head is floating full of Sanskrit footnotes.

Then there was a judge in California who decided that these five students of Moon's were head-copped, and he declared them incompetent, gave them to their folks, and their folks got to send them to this farm where they send you to get your head back. Then that was reversed a few weeks later because some other judge, a higher judge, said,

"That looks perilously close to locking people up for a difference of opinion, depriving people of their civil rights for difference of opinion."

Even our kids know where Moon is at. One of the kids had a dream about Moon the other night. They dreamed that Moon had Kimberly, man, and that I was going to go get Kimberly back. It penetrates into the consciousness to the level where eleven and twelve-year-old kids say,

"Wow, man, what if Moon got Kimberly? Would Stephen go get her back?"

In all charity, I hope that the inevitable karma that Moon reaps from overloading his scene with so much dishonesty that it collapses, would just hurry up and get on with it. You understand, this is not wishing him any bad luck. He's having worse luck while he's copping all these people's heads than if he weren't so successful, for *his* soul.

It's really kind of unfortunate to be too fast of mouth and too fast of head to ever have to listen to anybody else. There's a few folks wandering around like that. But the reason Moon is doing his thing is that nobody can take him. Maybe you'd have to learn to speak Korean to do that, anyway. Or do you have to take his interpreter first?

Some of the evidence that was put up to show that these people had lost their minds was that they had changed their ways, and that they were all different, and not at all like they used to be. They hardly seemed like the same person. I'm sure that's true. But I've read another report of almost exactly the same thing. There's this dude going down the road, and he stopped in a blacksmith shop, and he was messing with the horse. All of a sudden, something that had been said to him several days before, hit him so hard that it completely flashed him out, dropped him on his back, and he changed his name to St. Paul and was a completely different man, and people didn't recognize him any more, he was so different. Something had happened to him—he changed, man, he was *weird*. Well, wasn't he? If there was any truth to that tale at all, wasn't it something like that? So we are in a really, really delicate area.

Let me tell you a story that is sort of funny. I decide things sometimes on the basis of principles that are way back up in there, rather than just the immediate factors. Like in the early days of the Caravan, when I decided that I didn't want to wear a chicken's foot peace symbol around my neck, it was not because I disapproved of the peace symbol or anything like that. It was that I knew something about primary and secondary symbols, and that if you put a secondary symbol in the place of a primary symbol, it makes folks uncomfortable, and they wonder where you're at. So I said,

"Let's don't. We're peaceful; we're draft dodgers; we just ain't going to wear that chicken's foot. It's a secondary symbol, and I don't want to clutter up our thing with a secondary symbol."

So then we got over to the Martin Farm, and a fellow came up from a shopping news journal down in Alabama, about fifty miles south of us. He came and did a little story on the Farm, and he went around and dug the Farm, and we were pretty rudimentary in those days, but he liked us okay. He saw we were trying. And he went back home and wrote his story. He also gave me a previous issue of his shopping news, so I could see what his thing was like. And in that shopping news, there was an article about how this guy had wondered where the chicken's foot peace symbol had come from. Upon researching it, he found that symbol appearing on the devil card of the Tarot—the one with all the horns and stuff. Then he checked further back, and found that it was an old witchcraft symbol from the Middle Ages. Now, Tennessee and Alabama are in Fundamentalist territory, and he said the chicken's foot had to do with satanism. And then, when I got the next issue of the shopping news, it pointed out that he had noticed that nowhere on the Farm was the chicken's foot displayed. How about that? It's not like I knew that was going to happen or anything, but I just didn't want to be putting up a secondary symbol in the place of a primary one, because I knew that somebody would not like it. I knew that something in your mind understands that, and knows that you don't worship secondary things, no matter what they are.

Another aspect of consciousness in today's society is programming, and de-programming. Programming is a word you've heard all your life when you listen to a lot of radio _programs_, television _programs_, which are called programs because they're figured out earlier, and then run past you. There is a _program director_, who figures out what the program is going to be.

There are also computer programmers, who figure out what the program's going to be for a computer. If a computer is going to do a complex piece of figuring, you have to tell it what to do, because a computer isn't really smart; it just counts on its fingers fast, and you have to tell it what to do. So that's its program, the instructions of what to do. And then you put the program in one place, and the information in the other place, and the computer does the operations in the program to the information.

Now, when you hear these people talk about they're going to de-program somebody who's been in a Moon camp or a Hare Krishna community or whatnot, when they talk about de-programming, it means that *they are assuming that these people have been programmed,* the way you program a computer—that someone has figured out everything they're going to do, a program, and then they do that. And that is what the parents and the people are objecting to, and that's why the de-programmers that are working out of Arizona make ten thousand dollars a head. Bounty hunters, bounty hunters.

When we first came down to Tennessee, we went past a little church over in Columbia, which says, "Free Will Baptist Church." And as we came past that, I said,

"Hot dog! Free will. Somebody here's in our church."

Right now we have been fortunate enough to have only been peripherally touched by this. There's an article in a ladies' magazine that talks about de-programming, and goes through a list of ten or so communities, and we're right smack in the middle of it. But it's just two words, "The Farm," and most people are such bad readers that they'll probably miss it anyway. But nonetheless, we have been linked in that fashion. And it's kind of funny, because when that happens it means it's almost out of my hands.

I've said in the past that I thought there were people who didn't look at me deeply enough to understand the difference between me and Sun Moon. I really want anyone who is one of those folks, or thinks he might be, to dig in and find out what I mean by that. I'd hate to have to make anyone move on just on account of that, but it would be so dangerous to have anyone standing around looking head-copped in my vicinity. I just am not at all interested in anybody being head-copped in my vicinity. *I want people to take good care of their gourds.* Because it's really out of my hands. From here it goes on to *By their fruits you shall know them.* And if Farm folks come on all thick-tongued and stumble-bum and can't do it, it's going to look bad.

But I think the strongest thing that we can do for everybody in the whole country who's involved in this question right now, is to lay it out on the line openly, and send it out and publish it out to everybody who wants to see it, and _let them read our books—in the sense of audit our books._ Because these are clean books. We don't allow no head cop here. Not institutional _or_ amateur.

There is a difference between copping and having your head copped. I think what copping is really about is not copping to a doctrine or to a person, but that you will get off of your own personal trip and look at the larger trip. That's what I really feel iike when somebody comes to join the Farm; they don't really necessarily have to be here a long time for me to know where they're at. Folks join the Farm, and I feel them just really solid, because it's like _they understand the situation._ The thing that is evident about the Farm, to businessmen especially, is that we all must want to do this real bad, or we wouldn't have been able to do it.

There is also a difference between freedom and license. License is granted from somewhere else. Freedom is only self-granted, for a start. And that's the difference in how you behave under freedom and under license. Under freedom, you know you are responsible for everything you do. Under what they call license— licentious behavior, and like that—you think you can do anything, because you're covered. But there is no such thing as license. You are responsible for what you do _anyway._ Whether or not somebody else lets you know _That's okay_ or says,

"This is cool to do that."

Most of the unusual religious groups in the country have a real high rate of turnover—if you just relax awhile, they'll come out of it. I saw a real nice letter to the editor by a lady who said that her kid had joined the Hare Krishna movement, and she didn't dig it, but she didn't do anything about it, and he stayed about three months, and then he left. And she said,

"I'm glad he's not in it, but he's a better person somewhat for having been in it."

She had to admit that she sees a little change in him. Well, that's what I wanted to bring out about the _community as guru._ Because there are all these specious doctrines that people keep falling for. And you say,

"How come people fall for such _dumb stuff?"_

There are various ways they fall for dumb stuff like that. One of them is bad religious educations, so they don't know any better. One of them is, maybe somebody showed them a whole lot of energy, and they copped to the energy without trying to find out what was behind it. Those are some ways people do that stuff. *And also because there's something there*—because if it was totally hollow, no one would stay. *What is in there?*

What is in there is the *community*, which is the reflection of the true guru on the earth. And that's why those things have some validity to them. That's why people go back to them, and that's why people stand up for them and defend them: because they found something in them.

I saw another letter from another mother who said that she had caught some documentary about a Moon camp, and that she liked how they were with each other. She liked how loving they were to each other. She liked that stuff, but she detested Moon, and felt that he was totalitarian and Nazi, and just had their heads in a grip of steel. And she said,

"How sad that there's not a way to have the love and the camaraderie and the cooperation and the friendship without the totalitarianism of it." That's not an outraged parent calling the deprogrammers. That's somebody really reasonable trying to understand where her kids are at. We have to, all of us, really make an effort to drop our old personal habitual hassles with our parents and welcome them into our hearts so that they all know they're welcome here, and that they can come see their grandkids anytime, and even spoil them a little.

People join, for instance, the Krishna movement, in good faith, and they say,

"I'm going to learn these practices. I'm going to try to learn how to stay high."

A lot of them are coming out of a place where they are going to give up their dope, going to learn to stay high on their own, and stuff like that. Very good motives in some ways, in the people who go into that kind of thing. And then they do the thing, and so they do what's appropriate. If you go to a zendo to sit, and they want you to shave your head, you'll probably shave it. So you have a bunch of people trying to do the thing, and here's the thing about the head-copping power of the cults and movements—*it ain't as powerful as anybody thinks. People are not that dumb; they don't get their heads taken that easy, and nobody has that fancy a mental technology.*

Another reason they're after the Moonies is because Moon said that you could lie for somebody else's good. Heavenly deception. That's another thing that makes people mad about his trip, because there is hardly anyone so unsophisticated as to think that ain't a backwards teaching.

One of the people who's talking about all the Moon brainwash practices is a dude who used to be an indoctrinator for Moon, and has talked to thousands and thousands of people for him in his name. And this dude checked out of the club, and now he's talking about what he used to do, and what a fierce programmer he was, and what a high percentage of them he got. And it doesn't matter whether he's working for Moon or against Moon, where he's really at is he's on this big ego trip about how many people he got for Moon, and how he is going to get them back. And it's about how his mind is going to get all these other people's minds, and _he_ is a head-copper. And when he left Moon, all he did was go independent. That dude talked about what a bad head-getter he was; and he just wasn't that bad. If all those people hadn't been just _hungry_ and _thirsty_ for something to put up with his obvious bullshit, to try to glean some truth out of what he said, there wouldn't be any people listening to him at all. And there ain't any big, bad head-coppers like that out there. I've had people try to go for my head in every way imaginable, including outright frontal assault from a well-known yogi, like going to look me in the eyes and hypnotize me right on the spot. I was amazed at the _chutzpah_, man, to come up and pull a number like that.

But you can demonstrate the existence of free will, even to someone who doesn't believe in it. The only one who knows whether you have free will or not is you, anyway; you're the only one who really knows if you're doing it like you'd like to do it, or close enough to be reasonable. Did you ever see one of those things in old Zen stories where a Zen student, for some apparent reason which you can't quite fathom, pops some Zen master in the chops and somehow seems to get away with it? That might have been a demonstration of free will. Just do your thing. Do your free will. You can't hardly argue about it; just do it.

Do your thing. Do your free will.
But be very careful that you're not inhibiting someone else.
You can't inhibit your old lady and not let her get out.
You can't inhibit your old man and not let him get out.
You can't inhibit your kids and not let them get out.
Everyone should be very careful and not inhibit anyone else,
And treat everyone else's free will like a
Sacred flower.

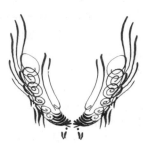

After Jonestown
in San Francisco

There was a wild time about a decade back there when San Francisco was like the basketball court, and we had the playoffs here. It was a pretty heavy trip for a while, and we learned a lot. We learned how information is transmitted from person to person about some very delicate, high stuff.

I believe that what went on in this area made a real difference in the world. It helped stop the war in Viet Nam, and it helped integrate the South. It was a powerful period of time that came from here.

There was stuff that went down involving hundreds of thousands of people in really large pieces of information and knowledge. Heavy stuff went down right here in this city. And we come around ten years later and look for evidence of that thing that went down, and say,

"Wow, they've almost covered it up in ten years. In only ten years, they've almost covered it up completely."

And then you really have to look again and examine the old traditions of the old monks who went off and tried to keep the knowledge alive through the Dark Ages, to really understand what we're trying to do. We're trying to keep a piece of knowledge alive for more than ten years, trying to pass something from generation to generation, perhaps. Maybe we can avoid having to make a fresh start every generation; maybe there can be enough trust and information and enough love between generations as to let us take that inertia and keep it rolling, and keep it moving. San Francisco has been the birth place of a lot of stuff.

The Farm took up television along with Watergate—when television got better. So we watch a little t.v. now and then. And right in the middle of the Jonestown thing, we caught an old *Star*

Trek rerun that seemed significant to us. Mr. Spock was walking across the control room of the *Enterprise,* and suddenly he groaned and dropped to his knees. Such behavior shocked everyone, in the normally imperturbable Mr. Spock. They said,

"Spock! Spock! What happened?"

He said,

"A shipload of Vulcans just exploded out there somewhere."

I think we all felt it just like Mr. Spock. It was pretty strong for us. How different from us? Not much. It was a heavy trip, and it put out a real strong vibe. So I came back to San Francisco because I knew the city had a strong knot on its heart.

We did a bunch of heavy stuff together before. There was the Monday night the students were shot at Kent State, and we had a long discussion about morality, revolution and violence. Folks came to Monday Night Class and said,

"We've got to get guns. They're shooting us."

I said, "No, no, you can't go violent. You can't give in. Knowing what we know is so precious that it would really muddy it up if we moved in that direction. We have to hang in there knowing what we know and don't muddy it up."

I feel really close to San Francisco. I've tripped here hundreds of times and came to really love the place. And sometimes it really seems like this place is just screwing up. Why does it seem like weird stuff happens in San Francisco? One of the reasons that weird stuff happens in San Francisco is that *a lot* of stuff happens in San Francisco, and you have a statistical percentage that a certain amount is going to be weird.

That's one of them. The other one is that folks in other parts of the country are just as weird; they just aren't as organized about it.

There is also the breakdown of the society, which we are currently witnessing. This is a society that is going into a certain form of decadence. The Federal government got a tremendous boost through World War II and all of the events that happened after that, until it reached a certain pinnacle of strength, at which point it is being rebelled against at large and small levels, all across the country. Some significant pieces of that go clear back to when Alioto made it so that the bridge fares were only to get *into* the City, and you could get *out* for free—underlining that it was the

Imperial City/State of San Francisco. It had seceded somewhat. And Jarvis' Proposition 13 is another states'-rights kind of trip where it takes power away from the government.

The thing that Brown wants to do about the Constitutional convention is another instance of bringing back the power from the government to the people. When you get down to states' rights, Brown seems to be as much a states'-righter as George Wallace. And so are a lot of other people right now, who say,

"Why should we send all this money to the Federal government, and they do dumb stuff with it and we can't talk to them, anyway?"

It doesn't seem rational, hardly. Why bother?

We seceded some years ago. That's part of what we are about. We seceded to this certain kind of non-profit corporation where you take care of yourself in this certain way and have a certain relationship to the government—which is as close as you can come to seceding without having the pony soldiers come to take you back.

Some people don't know about the Banana. Alfred Kahn, the President's ex-financial advisor, said,

"The President doesn't like me to call it a Depression. It makes him feel bad. So I decided to call it the Banana. Now, about the Banana that's coming, . . ."

So there's that to consider. The Great Depression. The guys that run the money machine have got it figured out to where you run the machine up and you can make a little money off it. They also have it figured out where they can run the machine _down_ and make some money off it. So they're just running the machine up and down, making a little money at each end, like a yo-yo. But entropy is sucking off the people, and they've almost run it up and down so many times as to break it.

They've been saying,

"Well, maybe we won't have a recession," or,

"Maybe this is only a recession."

When they say "recession," it means Depression. If they say "minor, infinitesimal slowdown," it means Recession. It's always one step worse than they tell you, in economic matters.

This Depression, I think, is one of many descending Depressions, and I think we're going to see some interesting things happening along through here. One that will be fun is when the oil-rich tourists from Mexico start coming up into Texas and buying rhinestone helicopters from Neiman-Marcus. This is going to change the country a little bit. When Mexico becomes a major heavy world power, and Socialist, right under our very nose, that's going to wig them out. That's some of the stuff that's coming.

America's position in the world is: this empire has fallen. But this empire is like a dinosaur that has just gotten the spitball behind the ear; we have to wait a few years for the tail to notice. It's already fallen. It fell a long time ago.

You knew it was falling when Rockefeller and Lindsay walked away from New York City and New York State.

They said, "Sure, you can have a Third World Congressman. You can have a lady Senator. Anything you want. Just let us get out from under before it collapses on us." And that's how things change hands.

It was kind of interesting. We didn't have to stop at the agricultural inspection station at the California border, because there wasn't nobody there. Can't afford it. Proposition 13 took it right off the map. That's the way it goes.

Without trying to be sentimental or funny or anything, the main thing I know towards understanding the events in Guyana is that Jim Jones lacked a teacher. He needed a teacher real bad. Because he embarked on a path, and to anyone who has studied, not just one religion, but many strains of religion, it's obvious that he made the first twenty-five, thirty mistakes that you make going out on that path.

He allowed people to put him in certain positions. People will put you in positions that you cannot accept. It's not,

"Well, I didn't tell them to do it."

It goes farther than that. It's that you have to tell them *not* to do it.

I could have rose petals under my feet. People have tried. I have not accepted rose petals under my feet. There is certain stuff like that that I have resisted. People who know me know that my path has been to try to study simplicity. You can't just tell yourself,

"Well, they come and give me everything, what can I do?"

What is moral to accept?

That is what I mean by making the first fifteen or twenty dumb mistakes down that line. He compromised himself again, and again, and again, and again.

He compromised himself politically, the way he used the political power of those folks. We could have been as opportunistic about the local power as he was with his. We could be giving them fits in Lewis County now; we have ten per cent of the vote in the county. In the elections in our district, where we have seventy-five per cent of the vote, we elected not to vote at all, because we felt like we had the handle so hard that we could put anybody in, and the other people who live in the district would have no choice about who represented them. Let them elect a constable to take care of them, and the Gate crew will take care of us.

Who was responsible for what happened at Jonestown? Subtract the free will of the people who should have knocked him on the head a few days earlier, and the rest of it is pretty much all his.

They used to tell us, ten years ago, that a false teacher can lead himself and all his students to hell. And we used to think, "Oh, one of those metaphors."

Unh-uh, ain't one of them metaphors. The old religions are old maps and charts about navigating in territory where what you are and what you really believe _happens,_ where you manifest your future in front of you. He manifested a paranoid future that had no substance in it. It couldn't go anywhere. It was too paranoid. It had to cease. There were two classes of people—one with guns, and one without. That would tend to make anyone suspicious.

He tried to get in contact with me a year and a half before that happened. He sent me letters, a lot of brochures, newspapers and stuff like that. The newspaper was all full of this-one's-out-to-get-us, that-one's-out-to-get-us, here's-another-one-out-to-get-us. It was so incredibly paranoid that I made a note to the person I was doing the mail with, saying,

"File this. Don't answer. Don't even let him know we got it, but file it and watch."

I'm sorry. Real sorrow. But he couldn't have done it to those old and black people if they had not been softened up by this society, if they were not terrified by the coming Depression and being on a fixed income and not really knowing how to do it. They had been softened up by the dependent position that they are in, depending on a government that is capricious and can change its mind and they were softened up by the society to that degree, that's how you can do some of that. If they had been really fiercely independent citizens, how could he?

There's also a thing about it being a sign of the times. A friend of mine who has a newsletter pointed out that having the kids crawl underneath their desks and pull their dresses over their heads for atomic bomb peril is a kind of suicide drill, too.

The Eye of Conscience

When they say someone has a bad conscience, that doesn't mean that it don't work right. It means it's working good. That's why it's bad.

That *con-* is Latin for "with." Then the second part, *sci-*, is like the *sci-* beginning of science and those kind of words. So *conscience* means something like "with knowledge."

Your mind is a perfect computer. If it weren't, you wouldn't be able to get out of bed in the morning. It works. No matter what your expediencies, or what you're driven to do, or what you do in excesses of need, or what you do in excesses of self-indulgence, part of you is sane and is keeping good notes, is paying good attention and knows what's going on. That is your conscience. And it's right there and it *always knows.*

Ain't anybody that I know who don't got one of those.

Conscientious. I really wanted to define the word *conscientious* well, so we really understood what it meant, so I could use it.

We need to teach our kids to be conscientious objectors. If it comes to doing a draft, they say,

"There are some guys who object who we aren't going to pay any attention to because they ain't conscientious. But if somebody comes up who is conscientious and objects to this war or to this Draft . . ."

Now they're talking about bringing back the draft, so the question of conscientious objectors is becoming more relevant to more people. This country has been gradually getting a little more civilized about that sort of thing. In World War I, they shot conscientious objectors. In World War II, I saw them locked up in prison camps, in the same camps with the German prisoners of war who were being brought back from North Africa. You had guys from Rommel's Afrika Korps locked up in the same prison camp with guys from Cleveland who didn't want to go to war.

Then they said certain religious groups were exempt—the Quakers, Jehovah's Witnesses, Mennonites—folks whose names you've got to respect because they pioneered not going to war in this county. The Quakers got it down cold enough that you could go to the draft board and say,

"I'm a Quaker," and they'd say,

"Oh. Conscientious objector."

And they'd give you your conscientious objector status.

But there's a breakdown of the family, folks traveling, church membership sliding and lapsing, not many people hanging to church any more, and you've got a lot of guys going in to the draft board and they say,

"I don't want to go."

"What church you belong to?"

"Well, I don't belong to a church."

"Well, you've got to go."

It's a question of religious freedom. If you could only have conscientious objectors that came from certain established religions, you had the freedom of religion question with the agnostics who might be . . . And then they looked for a word . . . agnostics who might be *conscientious*. So they created the class of the conscientious objector, just for us.

In a way, part of me almost wishes they'd try a draft. If they think all the old civil rights retreads are coming out for the nukes, just try *that* and see what you get.

Memory is related to conscience. Memory is another one of those automatic perfect systems like your blood pressure or your digestion or something that does its thing without you having to consciously do it.

The kind of tapes you cut when you're observing is the stuff your memory's made out of. The control on input to your memory, is the kind of observer you be. So if you be a very emotional observer, that'll color the kind of stuff you file, or if you be very wrapped up in one particular subject and don't pay attention to much other stuff, that will make the kind of stuff you file be a certain way.

I think the way to do that is to be open to all the possibilities, to be like a good scientist, like an Eagle Scout scientist in your observations: try to make real clean observations, and make them real fair, and try to allow for how other folks are, and just cut real nice tapes. It's like making the stuff coming at you be more clear. And then, a little bit down the line, the stuff that you've been cutting good tapes on will be your immediate fresh memory past and it'll be clearer and sharper and it will allow you to see farther. When you're standing in cleaner, better-built memory you can see farther.

Real pacifism is based not on the rule of some established religion or organization, but on a true understanding of conscience. If our children have to become draft resisters, they should understand their religious and philosophical underpinnings well enough that they can communicate them well enough that they won't have to go. We need to transmit it to our children in a very serious way, because if it's communicated correctly, it works. Nobody I ever counseled about going into the Army, ever went.

I said at one time that I was glad I wasn't of draft age during World War II, because it was such a brutal war of conquest being carried on by Germany that it would have been hard to know how to think about it without getting in it. That's the last war we had where people joined much. Mostly people haven't joined any wars lately—they usually have to drag them kicking and screaming.

Part of it was stirred up by the American propaganda machine, to fan people's emotions and get them hot; but part of it was truly horrifying stuff coming back from Europe. It was something big, it was like the twilight of the Gods. All civilization was going down. Germany had taken France. Italy was already in league with them. They'd taken the Netherlands, and gone up into Norway and Sweden and Denmark. The only country they didn't run through was Switzerland, because Switzerland was holding the bank. But they ran right through the other neutral countries, and it was an incredible thing to see. It was quite obvious that if he continued, and if he was able to pull off the kind of game he was trying to pull off, that he was going to jump off on the rest of the world. That was even his plan. The dude was really crazy and really powerful, and thousands of people believed the stuff he said.

We opposed that; and we got a little bit like it, from opposing it. Our FBI used to be the alcohol agents, the revenooers, before that; and then they became the super-snoopers, the secret cops. And we came up with the CIA and all that. By opposing that thing, we stopped it; and we became a little bit like it, too.

Consider what it would be like if the war situation in the world got so bad that Detroit quit making new cars for four years in a row. That happened. 1941 was the last new car they made; and they didn't make any new cars until 1946. Well, who cares about new cars? But as an example of how panicked was the economy, and what was going on, and the state of the nation at that time, it's something to think about. All the car factories turned to making tanks and jeeps and guns. Typewriter companies were making guns. Everybody in the country was making war stuff. And it pulled us out of the Depression of the 1930's.

That's what makes a lot of people feel kind of funny today. It pulled us out of the Depression; and as we go along here, skirting along the edge of *this* Depression, people who are old enough to remember that, become fearful. People wonder if they'll jump us off in another big one to cure the Depression.

Suppose it were that clear an injustice—Lord knows there's injustice in the world, just look at what Idi Amin was up to. And we know that those who live by the sword, die by the sword; but it's sometimes hard not to wish God to hurry up. You get that kind of stuff in your heart, and you have to handle it properly; because that's the impulse that comes out *war* on the other end.

But I don't think the issue would be that clear now. It's a question of the weird and inner subtleties by which the United States' chickens come home to roost. They didn't really conquer the world; they just let the multinationals do it for them. And the multinationals technically don't belong to anybody; they're just multinationals. But they belong to all the rich people who live in the United States.

That's why I think we need to try to pass along to our kids the impulses that made us pacifists. I was made a pacifist in various places, like Marine Corps boot camp, and foxholes in Korea. But that's a hard way to go; and if I'd had better sense, I never would have gone. And if anybody had ever pointed out to me that it was _courageous_ not to go, . . .

I was well conditioned. Locking up conscientious objectors and saying you had to be a Quaker or a Jehovah's Witness or something like that made it so you couldn't really go in as a matter of conscience and say,

"My heart forbids me to kill."

You couldn't go in and explain yourself as a matter of conscience; you had to come in behind an established religion. But we're religious revolutionaries. We're reestablishing the privileges of religion outside the establishment of religion. We have reestablished matters of sanctuary and conscience which do not belong to the law and do not belong to any establishment: they belong to the people. That's the sense in which we are religious revolutionaries and spiritual revolutionaries—_we try to return those things to the people that belong to the people._ Some things do not belong to the government, or any organization with mailing lists—they just belong to the people, under the Ninth Amendment to the Constitution:

> _The enumeration in the Constitution of certain rights shall not be construed to deny or disparage others retained by the people._

Being a spiritual revolutionary means defining some of that territory. A lot of the major religions have been around for a long time. And religions get mixed up with economic entities and countries and nationalities, so they get involved in all the wars and trips. There's really a tendency to say,

"Them's the bad guys and we're the good guys."

In World War II, almost everybody who was fighting, was fighting directly for God. The Christian folks were fighting black magic; and the German belt buckles said _Gott mit uns._ The Jews said they were the Chosen People; and the Japanese were coming from a 3,000-year line of direct sun kings.

It's that strange concept of the Holy War. There's a word, _jihad_, which means "holy war" for the Arabs. And the Crusades were a holy war. Up down. Light dark. Holy war.

Holiness in our Times

Of all the people who have ever lived in the history of mankind on earth, *half of them are alive now.* Some people talk about that first Neanderthaler who got high and realized we were all One. I call him the primordial Buddha. And from the time of the primordial Buddha until now, in a progression you can see, as population increases in its progression, the crew you have at any step along the way is equal to the whole rest of the crew that built up to it. There have been nine or ten billion people in history. We have four and a half billion of us here, and it took about four and a half billion to bring us to this point.

Here's another piece: Did you ever hear the one about how we're all related to everybody? Here you are. You have two parents, four grandparents, eight great-grandparents, thirty-two great-great-great-grandparents, sixty-four great-great-great-great-great-grandparents, a hundred and twenty-eight, two hundred and fifty-six, five hundred and twelve, one thousand and twenty-four, ... and it goes on like that, and your relatives ascend in this big curve, up the family tree.

Now on the other hand, we have the people coming the other way, down through history from the primordial Buddha. You have someone there and he reproduces and his thing goes out, and splits in two, and he has some kids and his kids are half him and half his old lady, and their kids are half their old lady, and on down the line like that. So you have the one about your relatives going back up one way, and people coming the other way, and it makes a diamond. And at a point back in history, everyone shares common ancestors. Do you dig that mathematically? Hang on to that one.

Now here's another one. *Among all peoples, everywhere, there is a normal bell curve of distribution of intelligence and talents.* The normal bell curve of distribution is the one where you have a little curve that's shaped like a bell, and you have your real, real tall eight-and nine-footers at one end, and your real, real short three-foot and two-footers on the other end, and you have all the five-sixers and six-footers in the middle in the big bump. Same way for intelligence, same way for mechanical aptitude, same way for electronic skills. Any quality that you could determine among people, you would find distributed evenly all the way across the normal bell curve of distribution. So you now have a handful of people, four and a half billion or so, and the four and a half billion it took to get here. And among the four and a half billion it took us to get here, there is Moses, Christ, Buddha, Krishna, Zoroaster, Saint George, Saint Francis, all the saints, all the avatars, all the Holy men. Now, according to a normal bell curve of distribution, which we are told we have, *there should be among the four and a half billion people who are alive on the planet now, people who are as talented and as smart and as together as anyone you can name from past history.* Have I violated any logical or mathematical laws getting to this point? So we can therefore assume that, among the population of the planet now, there are walking around through it all the saints, all the martyrs, all the teachers, all the gurus, all the avatars—that, walking around among the four and a half billion now, according to the normal bell curve, we have those talents among us in the present crew.

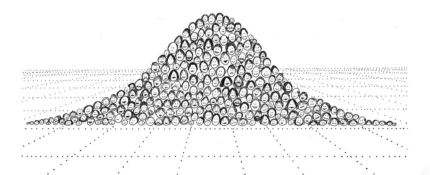

Religion is like the mechanics of how we deal with the phenomena of God and consciousness on an individual and planetary basis. And religions as institutions are to try to preserve their teaching, to try to save it for posterity. And we have lines of apostolic succession that come down to us twenty-five hundred years in the Buddhist, two thousand years in the Christian, twelve, fifteen thousand years in the Vedanta. One of the basic Christian beliefs is that when you be a Christian, you are plugging into an energy source that has a two-thousand-year-long extension cord plugged back into what was a guaranteed energy source, Underwriters' Laboratory-approved, good karma energy source. And there are a lot of people who say,

"Whooo. Hang on to the extension cord, man."

And I honor that, and it's true: that's good juice and it comes down that cord; it does do that, just like it said. However, according to that normal bell curve of distribution, _there exists good juice, good Holy energy that is common to our time frame, not just to past ones._

And, if you have the intelligence and the courage (and that's one of the nice things: you may not be able to just whomp up any intelligence right now, but if you whomp up some courage, it'll bring your intelligence up; you can whomp up some courage and it'll change _everything._) But you have to be discriminating, because the purpose of that two-thousand-year-long extension cord is for folks to have energy sources that are not going to lead them off into some kind of Never-Never Land and sink them in the swamp and lose them—it's supposed to be _good_ juice.

I think that the real proper practice of religion is a balance between honoring the old juice and recognizing the incredible dedication of trying to pass something hand-to-hand for two thousand years. It is also important to recognize that we live in the here-and-now, and we must have native, home-grown Holiness of our own—which comes from these hearts, which, according to all that math, are as good as any hearts, any time, anywhere. If not you, who?

The thing that was really common to Jesus Christ and Gautama Buddha is that _whatever they had was the people's._ Their consciousness was the people's. Now, it was Holy times then—that's one of the things we have to remember—and we've had some Holy times in our lifetime. It's pretty Holy now, but we just had a pretty wild trip happen about ten years ago. It got pretty Holy—*Hoo, haah!* Outrageous.

At first, people don't believe in magic. Then something happens, and they find out that magic is real. Some folks get scared at that point. They say,

"What happens if some bad dude comes along, a strong magician and everything, and magicks you, whips a spell on you? What do you do?"

Well, if you are in a situation and someone does a little magic in front of you and you see some magic happen, what you're supposed to do at that point is, *do some magic, too.* If there's enough ambient energy in the situation that *anybody* can do any magic, *everybody* in the situation can do some, too, if they have the courage to try it. Anybody can put a water wheel on Niagara Falls if they want to, within limits of the county planning commission and whatnot.

If you really study the old Scriptures, you'll see that it wasn't just one stoned consciousness walking around in an unstoned environment; there was a lot of heavy stuff going on all around, for a while. And the characteristic that was common to both Christ and Buddha is that they both had that real Bodhisattvic consciousness. According to what we are taught in the Scriptures, they had it knocked, they had it made. Jesus, we are taught, was the Son of God, could call legions of angels if He felt that was where it was at. And Buddha could command the king of Hell. Buddha died from eating some poisoned food, and Christ was executed like a criminal. How come? They had all that juice. All that energy, all that power, all that stuff. How come? *Because it would be wrong to use it just for your own personal self.* They used it for everybody, even up to where it came to their life and mankind's life. They were responsible with that incredible energy up to and including their own death.

Buddha is the prince of the Bodhisattvas, and Jesus is the prince of the Bodhisattvas; but don't you know that there's a lot of us over the centuries who have dedicated everything we've had? There have been a bunch of folks who said,

"Well, personally, I'm strong enough to hack all this—I could just go and take care of myself," who decided to say,

"No, I ain't going to do that. I'm going to stay here and be Florence Nightingale," or take care of the folks in the Black Hole of Calcutta, or one of those trips. Those folks are Bodhisattvas. They are One. And we can't separate them.

Somebody was asking about . . . _this season's people_, and wanted to know what it was I was trying to explain to them. I said, "It's a letter to a materialist, to try to crack them over."

What happened to us made it so we couldn't be materialists anymore. Now, that didn't mean we were home free. There was a multitude of weird disciplines that we could join from that point, but at some point _we were not materialists anymore_.

Sometimes I might criticize other teachers, just for the sake of keeping my amateur standing together, but basically, I disapprove strongly of, for instance, money-gathering techniques used by some groups who come up and grab a hold of you in the airports and that kind of jive. I think that is magic that shouldn't be used from people to people. It's a wrong thing to hit on people like that. But at the same time, I'd rather they have the bread than the military-industrial complex. I'd rather they have it than the war people.

Some people are very active psychically, and do a lot of magic, without really knowing it. There are a lot of kids who are accomplished magicians. They turn their parents inside out, _Abracadabracazap!_

"Make me a malted."

"_Zap!_ You're a malted."

So there are strong magicians who don't really have any idea what they're doing, or how they're doing it. But a lot of things happened to us when a lot of us were first stoned: we walked in and saw a lot of stuff like that happening:

"_Wow!_ Has this been happening all my life? Or did I just make it up for this trip?." That's why we kept going back again and again, to answer that question.

"Has this been going on all the time?"

"Yes, it's been going on all the time."

The psychic worlds are far out: they go along and do their thing, whether you pay attention to them or not. People in insane asylums have tremendously rich psychic lives. Wow, is it noisy in a place like that, on the head bands.

Many people have had misunderstood religious realizations. They feel the presence of the One, and, because they have not been instructed about this, they say,

"I am the One."

They lose the message that the One is so strong that if you are standing next to the One, the One is not going to say,

"I am Sam Kropotkin."

Sam Kropotkin is going to say,

"I am the One."

I have seen so much heavy stuff go down myself that I try to be very open-ended, and try not to say that nothing could happen, and try to make room for things to happen. But a lot of times, people who are in doubt get into things like,

"Okay, I'm going to flip this coin, make it come down how you want it."

God is not going to make you win the Irish Sweepstakes, or prove it to you in some way like that. You just have to say,

"Where did I come from?" Where did the scenery come from? Did you build it? Do you know who built it? What is it that you are doubting?

When you doubt, you only doubt yourself. You can't doubt the earth. You can't doubt the sky. You can't doubt grace, and you can't doubt intelligence. That would be like doubting rock. The thing that hangs people up in questions of doubt is when a specific person says they are going to do a specific number, and you're going to prove a specific miracle. Well, fancy stuff goes down. I believe it goes down within the laws of the system. I do not believe that miracles are outside the laws of the system. They're outside the laws of three-dimensional physics where people with their head in the sand teach it.

Doubt seems to be created by relative truth. Relative truth is as if you'd been swimming all your life, and had never touched bottom, and all you can do is paddle. And while you paddle, you can't take any side trips too seriously, so you have a provisional belief in everything. But it's just provisional—until I ever find out better, I keep paddling. *But if you ever went up close to the shore and felt the sand under your feet, you'd be another creature.*

It is that thing that changes you from having been flapping in the breeze all your life. When you're flapping in the breeze, it's best to deal with relative truth, because if you start taking relative truths and making them absolute, you can get like the Nazis. Many people are afraid of the real truth—they think that real truth is just a really stubborn fixation to a relative idea. _But there is absolute._ There is, for instance, absolute existence. Doubt our existence. Go ahead. If you could doubt our existence hard enough, you could make us go away. And you notice we don't. Here we are. What are you going to do about it?

Absolute truths are those truths which can be universally applied without doing injustices to some people to make something come out right. If you try to stick a relative truth down on a lot of people, it's like sticking a cookie-cutter down on them and cutting off everything that doesn't fit. The absolute truth is the real shape before the cookie-cutter got 'em—where they were really at. The truth that is self-evident, in front of you. And that's absolute.

Now, when you talk about that, you have to get a big enough viewpoint. There is local injustice. By and large, this species has been able to live on the rock for the last eighteen million years or so and survive, that is, we didn't wipe ourselves out. The only thing to say is,

"Well, here we are."

We have not been that nice. We have mostly survived by the power of, I would say, God, the innate wisdom of our biology, the innate wisdom of the Universe. We don't digest our food consciously, we don't grow our babies consciously. And that stuff happens—on God's automatic pilot. And the stuff you see that is God's automatic pilot is what has brought us through. The stuff that has been a hassle to us has been man, and man's ego, and man's greed; and to the extent that we become more in line with God and less in line with man's greed, then we go more toward a real norm. There is enough to go around _right now._

God and Godzilla

I read a Letter to the Editor the other day that said that most of the other nations of the world, or civilized countries, have some kind of a national health care, and that most of those countries with a national health care service have better health statistics than the United States does. It said that people who come from other countries to the U.S. are shocked and saddened and sickened to see what the American medical profession is doing to the people. His letter pointed out just that fact, that most other countries have some kind of a national health care, and that we are not up at the top of the statistics—we aren't that good. Childbirth statistics, operative statistics, all that kind of stuff. It was a pretty revolutionary letter. That letter was written by Edward Kennedy.

When Edward Kennedy gets to saying something like that, it's comparable to the time when Richard Nixon pointed out that in the United States, seven per cent of the world's population uses sixty per cent of the world's resources. He had to say that because it had been said about ten years previously, loud and long and by a whole lot of other people, until it percolated through the consciousness so bad that he had to say it. And that's where it's at with the statement of Kennedy's—that the hospital system stinks of the corruption and the greed. The medical establishment has become so vile as to become perceptible across national boundaries to other countries.

I was taught a lot by an Indian Swami whose name I've completely forgotten. He ain't one of the really famous ones, and I really don't know why not. But he was a Swami in India and he got into reading the *Bible*. He read that Jesus commanded his disciples to go forth and heal the sick and heal the blind and the halt and the lame, and this Swami didn't particularly know how to go *Zap!* and make somebody well, so he went out and he got himself a bunch of eye doctors and he started an eye clinic. He's given five or ten thousand free cataract operations now, and *he causeth the blind to see.* If penicillin is where it's at, it's a miracle; anything that works is a miracle. Whatever works is a miracle. *That it works is a miracle. That anything works is a miracle.*

The doctors have skills that are useful to know. But the thing about their fancy technology is that the most expensive technology they have is only supposed to be used in a minimal number of cases; but they make it standard so that, when you go in to have a hangnail removed, you have to pay for the presence of the anesthesia machine, and for this machine and that machine, even though you don't use them. The reason you have to pay for them even when you don't use them is that it is being done through the profit-making system. There is overhead to be considered, and profit, which are considered *at the expense of the patient,* who after all pays the bill one way or another.

I'm very serious about the medical scene in this country right now. I feel like it's a level of oppression where, if you saw some dude on the late television movie, riding along on his chariot throwing sheep bones and garbage over the side, and running through the people's flocks and fields and tromping down the wheat, you would say,

"Hey! When is Spartacus going to come get him?" or whoever it was, whatever time frame the movie was in. You'd wait a little while, and the hero would come do it.

As much as I've watched in the last few years of having to be intimate with the health care of all of us, being connected to it and watching the level of arrogance and uncompassion and unfeelingness and greed and ritual dishonesty that I have seen among doctors, that the doctors we have seen who are honest are in the rare, rare minority. It is a pleasure—we know one in Wisconsin, one in Iowa, one in Rhode Island, a few in Tennessee, one in New Mexico, a few other states. So I'm not saying that I'm down on the medical profession, but I don't really think we should be denied access to their goodies.

I read a beautiful explanation the other day by a Filipino Jesuit, Juan Mateos, and it gives a good picture of how Jesus stands with the people. Juan Mateos says you don't have faith in Jesus about salvation, _which is sure,_ but that you help Jesus with His work to change it for all of the poor of the world: that Jesus stands with the people, and if you aren't standing with the people, you aren't standing with Jesus, because that's where He stands.

Now this happens to be written in English, and if I were speaking Sanskrit I might use another word when I came to Jesus, but it wouldn't make any difference. My visions have been without name, but of impeccable credential.

Juan Mateos talks about the relationship of Jesus to the people of His time, and he points out that Jesus wasn't anti-Semitic or anything like that—He was Jewish Himself—but what He was fighting and what He gave His life against was not any group of cultural people. He was against the power that goes with wealth and social position in any ruling class, in any culture, in any country, in any time, in any age. The very interesting thing about Juan Mateos' story of the life of Jesus is that it comes to the point where you could almost replace where it says the Jews and the Jewish elders and the Sadducees and the Pharisees and names like that, with the Christians and the Catholics and the Baptists and names like that in this century, and it would read about just as good. A whole lot of the heavy money of the military-industrial complex has Christian stockholders. And Christians who do that are idolators. They are heathens, poor, ignorant, superstitious people, misled by ambitious preachers. That's what I think in my heart of hearts.

Jesus' church was never an exclusive social club. He said, "Be ye fishers of men." An open-Gate policy.

The hospital system is largely the product of the Protestant work ethic, and the more I learn about it, the more I see how people are victimized by it. I saw a birthing flick one night on television. It showed a young Puerto Rican lady in New York, idealistic as all get-out, who was going to do a natural childbirth. She went to her Lamaze classes. Then, when she went into the hospital to have her baby, they wouldn't even let her have a labor coach. She talked to somebody off-camera and said,

"Pretty strong, no?"

And they didn't answer her. The camera was there, and she just looked straight ahead and held her expression plain, and waited. Then she had a few rushes. Her rushes stopped, and then this doctor came in and examined her. She screamed while he examined her. I've seen a lot of ladies examined in all phases of labor, and I've never seen it cause anyone to scream. I've seen a few where it got them off pretty good—they dug it, it was nice and they said "Ahh," and made noises like that. But this lady screamed and fought because this guy came on to her so fast and so yang— head of obstetrics at this particular hospital. And he left her there, crying and screaming, and turned and looked into the camera and said,

"This woman is not in labor." And he walked away, and ordered her up for a c-section.

This was presented as an example of a relatively normal hospital birth. And it looked to me like the evidence in a malpractice suit. But I ain't an easily-snowed Puerto Rican lady from New York who doesn't speak very good English and is afraid to talk back. And I don't care if they don't like me or think I talk too much when I speak in behalf of the poor. I'll speak up for them, and it gives me strength, because I know who I'm speaking for, and why I'm speaking. There isn't anything conceptual about it. I don't want to sue individual doctors for malpractice; I want to see national medical health care all the way across the country.

The highest suicide rate, broken down by profession, has dentists, doctors, and chemists as the top three. That proves to me that the system is so corrupt that it's killing them, too: that it's so wrong that it's corrupting those folks, and that those folks need to be out of that system and into one that is not a money-based system. They need it as badly as the folks who are having to pay the money do. It corrupts an essentially human and free open love exchange by putting money into it.

It's not just the doctors. I know of my acquaintance one honest lawyer. Joel is the only honest lawyer I know. He has a legal crew, and I believe the rest of his crew is honest, too; but they haven't passed the Bar in this state. He is technically the only lawyer we know who is honest. But I think that a lot of lawyers are sellouts. The lawyers, in being the go-between the defendant and the bar, have partaken of the social position of the bar until you need a lawyer to talk to a lawyer—because talking to a lawyer is talking to some aristocrat establishment.

I know I'm getting close, when I see rich relatives get uncomfortable. When I was up in Vancouver, we were having this thing about white sugar again, and I was talking about hating to see superstition about any subject, and that the amount of superstition that's happening about white sugar is about as unscientific as the Dark Ages. I said people put out worse vibes about white sugar—I had a lot of people moving with me and laughing and rolling.

I said,

"People put out worse vibes about white sugar than they do about ego, heroin, or the capitalistic system."

And when I said "capitalistic system," that room went dead silent. Everybody quit laughing and they all looked at me.

Now that sounds extreme, but Jesus said,

> _"It is easier for a camel to get through the eye of a needle_
> _than it is for a rich man to get into the Kingdom of Heaven."_

Is that an extreme-sounding statement? What I see is that lawyers have no sense of justice whatsoever. Their minds have been destroyed in college. They've been taught to defend either side of the question without respect for the moral implications of it. They've been taught no truth, relative truth.

There was a beautiful lady at one of my trials who was the court reporter, and she was straight with me. She sat there and talked with me soft, just between me and her, while she was doing the court reporting. I'd be sitting there and they'd be doing me up, and she'd look up and say, real soft,

"You okay?"

And I'd say,

"Yes. I'm okay."

She's the one who said,

"Well, the liars is here. (Some people call them lawyers; but I call them liars, myself.) The liars is here!"

A Visible Spark

I can tell when it gets to be summertime, because I get a certain sort of mail from all over—people writing me about how much trouble it is for them to remember where they're at and keep their head together with everybody running around looking so beautiful in the summertime. One guy writes and says,

"I don't know, I just find myself looking at a lot of ladies' bottoms. I don't know, maybe I have sexual subconscious."

Love and lust and sex and tantra and electricity and communication and telegraph and radio are all sort of an ongoing, all-the-time thing in our minds. It just seems in the summertime it flares up, when everybody ain't got their macinaws on, and you can see what they look like.

The way you think about that kind of thing depends on how much information you have about what's going on. Now, I've said before that I believe that if you really understood energy well, you wouldn't get uptight at somebody who patted your bottom in the elevator. You might want to tell him to mind his space, which is your privilege to do, but you really don't have to be uptight or to think that it's strange, or so weird that you can't relate to it, or anything like that. There ain't anything so strange or so weird that you can't relate to it. I make that observation from my own case, in which I don't find anything so strange or so weird that I can't relate to it, and I don't really think I'm that much different than anyone else is.

Some people wouldn't understand it.

"How can somebody come up to somebody they don't know? How can somebody come up and violate my privacy?"

They say that nature abhors a vacuum. A vacuum is an unnatural situation, because the tendency is towards equilibrium. It's like lightning: when the cloud gets enough particles in it to charge one way and the ground has enough particles to charge the other way and there's this church steeple or tree or mountain, and they get close enough together, they will follow the laws of nature, and there will be an arc passed between them. If you find yourself in an elevator with somebody who's so lonely, has no friends and doesn't know anybody, who hasn't had any exchange of that kind of electrical energy with anybody for a long time, and you're kind of juicy, then it's like a cloud and a tree passing close together.

Now if everyone was all friends and introduced to one another in the elevator, it would be one sort of thing—

"Hi, ain't seen you for a while, nice to see you . . ." and you shake hands. Your arm is the material plane diagram of a piece of energy that goes back and forth between you. If somebody comes up and pats your bottom, their arm is just the visible spark of that lightning exchange of energy. It is that thing about that energy that has made the dress codes and regulations about how men and women are supposed to meet. How people are supposed to behave in public has been derived out of how to handle that kind of energy for thousands and thousands of years-millions.

So a fellow writes and says he has trouble, finds himself looking at ladies' bottoms. Well, most of the time, your eye is the pointer with which you mark where your attention is. It's like pointing a flashlight beam, or a laser: your eye marks where your attention point is. That's not just an optical phenomenon that takes place between your eye and that which it looks at; but your eye is a transceiver like radar: it puts something out, and it gets something back when you look. There are things you can look at that have no energy in them: you look at them and it isn't good to look at them, and you look away because it drains your energy to look at them. There are also things to look at that are so good, full of life force, so juicy and so full of energy that they attract your attention just like the strike of a match attracts your attention in the dark woods.

Your eye, and your mind, and your attention are as naturally drawn to see that little flash, that representation of energy—as naturally as the moth is drawn to the lamp. It is not a value judgment to find your eye passing that way. The value judgment is what happens inside your head. If you look and say,

"How beautiful! How good of God to turn me on to look at such a nice one," or if you're saying,

"Well, actually that one looks a little better than the one I have at home, I wonder if there's any chance," or,

"Mine used to look like that when I was younger," . . .

That's about being attached.

The fellow who writes me about the problem said he explored and introspected further about this question, and found that some young girls did it, too; and when he pursued that farther he found that young boys did it, too. He was drawn to beauty, and saw this beauty, and it moved his heart and he said,

"I wonder if I'm weird."

And he ain't.

There is communication in touch, and the distinction is what you say in your message. Possible messages could be like,

"Ah, you're nice and I love you and my heart goes out to you, it's nice to see you." Letting someone know you think they're a turn-on is an inexpensive present, but very nice. Letting little kids know they're a turn-on makes them grow. Letting old folks know they're a turn-on makes them live longer. I played excellent kneesies one time with a ninety-three year-old lady. She was goooood.

Your message might be that, or it might be,

"This is pretty good, and not only that, if you step behind the soy dairy with me, it'll get a little better." I'm sure we have all been in on those kinds of communications. They immediately tend to make you assess your relationships with everyone you know.

The whole question of being into touch as a mover of energy and as a communication is a central thing. Most people really know some stuff about energy. They know it because they do it; but they've never _thought_ about it, because they've kept that level of their life—as most people do—mostly subconscious. Now, it's real energy, and there are ways it can be moved. It's like electricity. You can have an empty battery and a full battery, and you can put down a trickle charge between them. You have a small passage to allow a small amount to pass, some way of restricting it so it doesn't all pass at once, and you let it trickle in. You can pass that energy over a period of time, or you can have the kind of energy where you can *Zap!* send lightning bolts over there and send it all over in one big chunk, *Bang!*

You can also modulate the energy in various ways; that is to say, you can put flavors on it. I had really fine communication with Ina May's mother one time where she was mad at me, which was usual, and I was sitting talking to her holding her hand, and trying for some human communication, and she was just being a chunk of Velveeta cheese in my hand.

I came on like,

"Eh? Eh? Are you in there? Are you in there?"

And all of a sudden, her hand turned electric—full of communication and full of information and very lively. She just spoke a short statement to my hand, of,

"Here I am and I am awake and alive and paying attention and listening to you on these channels,"

Then she let go of me and took my hand by the loose skin on the back of it and picked it up between her thumb and forefinger, and dropped it over on the bed. I had to cop that, not only did she talk that language, but she knew how to say heavy things in it. I was grateful for the communication, but a trifle blown, too.

Another thing about passing energy is that it can be passed between people on the basis of how much muscular energy is put into the transaction. If a couple of people hug each other with thirty-five pounds of pressure, a certain amount of energy passes; and if they hug each other with fifty pounds of pressure, there will be more energy passed. It's just that simple: if you put more energy into it, you will hot up the communication and make more energy flow. That's one of the variables that exist. It's like when you saw your old long-lost and he just cracked your back and about squashed your ribs. And with a strong amount of energy put into it, you can make a strong amount of energy pass between you.

Or, instead of the bear hug, you can have a touch at the tip of a finger with an unmistakeable statement or an unmistakeable question, and transfer the same amount of energy as a big bear hug in just a little tickle. The same amount of energy can transfer because you make agreements with people. Every time you touch somebody, you tell them in touch where they're at with you, and it can mean a lot of things.

I heard Suzuki Roshi was dying and we had a 400 cubic-inch Buick Wildcat medical car—the Farm's only car that ran in those days—and I took it and left for California, going as fast as I could go. I had tossed a picture of Suzuki up on the dashboard, and it landed on the dash in such a way that it reflected right up and was just like him sitting there out in front of the car, and I was looking out through his eyeholes down the road.

I charged down the road, man, haulin', and got to where he was, and got to the door.

The gateman didn't want to let me see him, and I didn't want to push. I'd just been driving three thousand miles as hard as I could roll, so I had a lot of inertia and push.

Richard Baker came around the corner and recognized me, and I had such an obvious rush on that he stopped and dropped me a _gassho_, real slow, to see if I was too fast to notice that or not, and I slowed down and gave him one back. He said,

"What's happening?"

I said,

"I heard Suzuki Roshi's very sick and I've just come from Tennessee to see him, and I would like to see him if I could, but I don't want to make him no hassle, and it's okay if I can't."

He said I could. I was so grateful.

I went up and I went to Suzuki's room. He was small and frail and very yellow, and he looked different than I'd ever seen him before. He looked regal. Royal. Very skinny and very pale and very puny, very weak and very yellow and very royal. I saw him and my heart went to him and I went running across the room. I reached out and he took my hand, and it just stopped me cold in my tracks where I was.

He couldn't have weighed more than seventy-five pounds or so. But he had so much power and command in his grip—it was like hitting a stone wall,

Clank!

It wasn't like he didn't want me up close; it was just that he wanted to stop me until he could integrate me for a minute. He just held me off a little until he integrated that hammer-down-for-3000-miles attitude I'd come in with.

He touched my hand three times that day, and each one of them said a different thing. One of them was just like you ran up too fast on a sword-master and suddenly found yourself facing the edge of his blade, while he figured out who you were. The next time he touched me he drew me closer to him, and that was very full of love and very intimate. The last time he gave me his hand it was like maybe when the Pope puts his ring out to you—regal again. And the most of what he told me was in touch. I hardly remember any of his words.

There are some free-love communities in places like Europe that you hear about now and then, basically a community organized around their genitals. I think that's because they're so repressed. In Europe it's been so repressed for so many thousands of years that they really have to break forth extremely to feel like they're getting out at all. But when people see the kind of promo they put out—like seventy-five people struggling in a heap—it's not necessarily from the viewpoint of,

"Oh, ick, they shouldn't be doing that 'cause it's so nasty," but it's an instinctive thing of saying,

"Oh, if you throw all of the subtleties and relationships together into one big old thing like that, you're going to lose a lot of the goodies—a lot of the subtleties and a lot of the love and a lot of the real things that are supposed to happen." It's not a matter of ain't-supposed-to-have-none-of-that-stuff; it's just not a very good way to go about it; it just reduces everything to its lowest common denominator of struggle. What about all the different kinds of love that pass between us? What passes between the midwives and the ladies that give birth is real love, electricity, gotta-feel-good kind. If it doesn't, the babies don't come out as good.

I say sometimes that I'm a tantric yogi, and I realize that's a hangup to umpty-ump million people in the world who don't have the slightest idea what that means. But I say that because it's shorthand for trying to say that I understand energy, life-force energy, how it runs between grownups and babies and people and animals.

This energy has to flow among us in a lot of different ways. A bunch of people get together and push a truck, and all their auras brighten up from that expenditure of energy. Their auras interpenetrate and pass energy among them. And when you work together in the field, and when you try to figure it out together in the offices, those people are being energetic, too. Energy passes head-to-head, body-to-body, bottom-to-bottom; and those people who think together also make love. And, as everyone knows who has ever been served food with loving hands, preparation of food for someone is making love, whether it's a barrelful or a teacupful; and the energy goes into it and passes along.

"Love one another" is one of the commandments, and some

folks take that commandment so seriously as to get themselves all out of shape behind it. But minds interpenetrate and make love. You have to have the agreement of that consciousness; you have to have the agreement of that free will. It is considered immoral to take a lot of energy off someone who isn't of age of consent—old enough to know what they're doing.

There are different ways energy can pass between people. If you be angry at somebody, you take their energy. It's not a good exchange, either; because you not only take it from them, but after you get it, you lose it from being angry. It's really a losing transaction for everybody. And you *can* move energy that way: You can scare somebody and move the energy. But the best way, and the only way that's kind, is to move it with love.

We have a whole set of interlocking agreements about how we move our energy together among ourselves. Some folks say,

"I like to move my primary energy in one place, but I want to be friends with other folks."

But it becomes evident that the seriousness or heaviness of an event in those energy levels doesn't have anything to do with the subtlety of the stimulus.

I fall in love with folks, sometimes two or three a week. It doesn't lessen the blow any—it's a heavy trip all the time—but what can you do in one lifetime, and how much karma do you want to cause? And so you say,

"Well, even though I fall in love with somebody, . . ."

That means you have some free will in the relationship; you're not just steered by astrology or something; so when you get with somebody you have to start using your free will on purpose and say, Okay, I choose to put my energy into this relationship, and try to bring it to fruition, and in order to do that, I will avoid starting such other heavy relationships that they will tend to make me unable to pursue this one to its fullest. Isn't that telepathic back in there in the marriage contract? You fall in love with someone; but you don't just go and disconnect all your energy and drop it on that person and say,

"Well, I used to be in love with so-and-so, but now I'm in love with you. . . ." This way lies madness.

Jesus says, "In Heaven there is no giving or taking in marriage. In Heaven, all people are similar to Me."

He didn't mean they were all men because He was biologically male; He meant that in the Heaven worlds, the shape of your body didn't necessarily mean anything. In the real highest energy exchanges we are all One, and we just go from soul to soul and it doesn't matter. But in the physical plane, which is below even the psychological plane, in both of those planes you have memory and karma and results of your actions and free will, and you have to be very careful and very kind and very full of love, which means very moral about how you arrange those energy relationships. You don't say,

"I'm in love with so-and-so, and I'm going to alienate their affections from so-and-so else so I can have him."

You honor other people's relationships.

It's the subtlety and the depth of the way we love each other that makes it possible for us to have a lot of love and a pretty clean mind. That's really a blessing, to be in a lot of love and a pretty loving situation, and able to have a pretty clean mind.

Cleaning the Terminals

In thinking about human electricity, I realize that there is human electricity, and there is human electronics. In the material plane, you have to make a distinction between electricity and electronics. Electricity is about the movement of energy from here to there, and the changes you put electricity through—like making it more powerful, alternating current, direct current. Electronics is another field; it takes the electricity and not only moves it around and makes it more powerful, it modifies it, and flavors it. Electronics makes for flavors of electricity, not just electricity.

In that way, depending on what part of your electricity you are talking about, people can resemble a storage battery, a capacitor, or a radio. The battery is a phenomenon of electricity. The original kind of battery was a box lined with metal, and a plug that went into the box, insulated so the plug did not touch the box in any way. Then, attached to that plug without touching the box itself was another piece of metal. Then you fill the box with a liquid acid, which becomes the only connection between the outer metal box and the inner metal piece hanging from the plug. So an electrochemical reaction takes place, and you can put one wire fastened to the box and the other wire fastened to the piece of metal in the plug, and you can touch those two wires together and get sparks. You get electricity right there.

A capacitor is almost as if you had a storage battery without the liquid. You can build an electrical potential up to a certain point, beyond which it would have to discharge. You can put juice in a battery over a period of time, and tap it out over a period; with a capacitor, you put juice in over a period of time, and you tap it out all at once, in one spark. People can do that, too.

But to contain a vibration, you don't have to be considered just as a battery or a capacitor. You can be considered as a radio, which is a standing wave of electricity. You create a wave, and you have it stand there. A stationary wave with a strong, definite shape. When you run electricity through that system, it creates a wave that stays the same. And you can modulate that wave, so it is the same as another wave somewhere else, and the waves will resonate together.

There is a difference between straight body electricity, transmitted by rubbing and touching, and electronic energy, which you do not have to touch because it transmits by radio. In the *Bible*, Jesus was walking down the road and suddenly stopped and turned around and said,

"Somebody touched me."

And they said, "What? What?"

He said, "Somebody around here touched me, got into my juice. Who is that?"

And a lady standing in the crowd said, "I saw you walking past and I knew you had a lot of Holy energy, and I needed to be healed, so I touched you as you went past."

He turned around to His disciples and said, "See? I told you somebody touched me."

He was a capacitor moving along through the crowd, and she just tapped Him out. It was cool with Him; He just wanted to keep the books: if He knew where it went, it was okay.

Now, you're supposed to be self-generating. You're supposed to be self-charging batteries. You can't just exchange energy from battery to battery. We're supposed to be able to charge ourselves. Actually, you don't really charge yourself; you just get pure enough and you are able to zap into bigger stuff and get charged from that. That's your thing.

It's almost the same in the material plane of electricity as in the spiritual electricity, because *we don't really know how much electricity there is.* The potential is infinite. The amount of electricity that we are sitting in right now is some millions or billions of volts. For instance, an electric generator has a core and a magnet, and it runs one of them around another and it generates a potential of electricity. The earth is eight thousand miles in diameter and about seven thousand miles of that is iron. And the moon is another chunk of similar kind of stuff, and here they are spinning around each other like a giant generator, and that creates an electrical potential which we here call zero. So we are living in a field of unimaginable intensity, which we just happen to be used to, spiritually as well as electrically.

When someone comes to an experienced mechanic and says,

"My battery is dead, and my car won't start", the mechanic doesn't immediately assume that the battery is dead. Even though he is told that, he doesn't assume that. He says,

"You check your terminals?"

The terminal is the place that is connected to the box, and the place connected to the piece in the middle. Those connections are the terminals. The mechanic knows that it is in the nature of electricity, because it is so powerful and electro-chemical in nature, that it tends to corrode the terminals. So you have to clean the terminals now and then, so they don't get corroded. In fancy equipment, you try to have terminals that don't corrode, like silver and other fancy metals.

And in people, when somebody comes to me and tells me,

"My old man or my old lady don't get me off no more, I think the battery's dead," I tell them,

"Check your terminals?" Which is, in human terms, your relationships. In most cases, we find not dead batteries, because if somebody really had a dead battery they wouldn't start at all. But love is so powerful and so heavy, and people are so incredibly complicated, made of beast and angel, God and ape, that love, strong by nature, can corrode the terminals if you are not careful.

For instance, back at the Family Dog rock 'n' roll hall in San Francisco when they were first trying to get it to be a rock hall at all, Chet Helms was running around San Francisco hustling as hard as he could, and his friends were helping him hustle in order to get this rock hall together. He had one friend who owned an old battered Cadillac limousine, so the dude with the limousine got himself a funky chauffeur's hat, and he started driving Chester around to make all his appointments with all the people he was trying to get together. So he would pull up in this black Cadillac limousine, and the dude, his friend with the chauffeur's hat on, would pop out and go and open the back door, and Chester would step out in his Afghanistan coat with white fur trim, carrying his snake staff, and go magic up a few partners for this rock 'n' roll bread. So he played this game with his friend—and in between appointments, they were turning on together, passing a joint from the front to the back seat of the Cadillac.

Then it started happening, getting it together, and Chester wasn't traveling too much, he was hanging out at the hall. But that guy liked that game, and kept wanting to do it. So he became the guard to the door to the Performers' Room. When you'd come into the Performers' Room, he'd give you a great sweeping bow, with a "Come on in, sir," and like that. And everybody was in the spirit of the game, and it was fresh, and they'd put a whole bunch of energy back into it, and there'd be a lot of juice in it for everyone.

Well, that went on for a few months, and after a while, people got in a hurry to see Chester, and that dude didn't quite put as much juice out as he used to, and it got to where he became a real one of what he was mocking. He just opened the door for a lot of people, who said "Thanks," and went on through and did not put full value into it—and he sort of almost fell out of love with the whole thing. It lost the form and the juice it had had before, and it came apart on him. He didn't really want to be obsequious to anyone; it wasn't what he had started out to do. And in the pressure of the game going on and on like that, they lost the spirit of the game, and he became sort of a servant, and he didn't dig it.

Suppose you get married, and you've been married about a week and one of you pops out of bed before the other and fixes a good breakfast and spreads it out and comes on strong that they really love you, and you come on strong how nice it is to be taken care of this way, what a groove, and I love you, too, . . . Boy, you'd better take care of it, and don't let it get worn down and make it pedestrian and ordinary and let the juice run out of it until it becomes something like,

"Toast, hold the coffee. Later, Baby."

So if the car doesn't start, you check your terminals. You have to scratch down through all the corrosions until you get to the bare, raw metal. When you're cleaning the human terminals, you have to get through all the corrosions until you get down to the quick. The way you can tell when you get down to the quick is someone goes,

"Ow."

And you say, "Oh. I got to the quick."

Then you know you have to back up and back up, and give room and give room, and try to open up and have no pride. Pride is one of the worst corrosions that can happen. It's mostly copper sulphate and lead breaking down in batteries; in people, it's pride.

Most couples who hassle for a long time, it's because they're prideful. One of them maintains their position and proves they were right.

"They did something to me, and I'm going to wait until they come through first. It was their fault and I'm going to wait until they apologize."

I feel like if I'm not straight with who I'm in love with, my ammeter is just way down in discharge as long as that situation continues. I don't want to sit and wait for some event to happen before I try to get that back up into the charge zone again. I want to start doing what I can do right now. If that means I have to say, I was wrong or dumb or,

"I'm sorry," or,

"Please forgive me," or,

"I don't care," or,

"I forgive you and it was okay, it wasn't heavy compared to what a heavy thing we're supposed to maintain between us," and don't lose it and hang on with that.

No pride, no pride, that's a place where nobody can afford a speck of pride.

A Miraculous Birth

I'll tell you a tale here. We've been having a difficulty with the charging system on the Greyhound. Either it won't charge enough to give the batteries any juice, or else it charges so much that it boils 'em dry. We've been working on this for a while.

The charging system is one factor in a very complicated set of circumstances. The way the air system works on the bus, is that if you have no air pressure, your emergency brake is on. You cannot take your emergency brake off until you have air pressure. That's another factor in the circumstances.

We stopped by the side of the road for a moment, and we tried to start up, and the emergency brake hadn't quite let off yet, and we stalled the motor. We said,

"Okay, we'll just start it up," and we went to start it, and we didn't have any juice in the battery to start it. So we thought,

"Well, what do we do?"

Albert, the electrician, decided we needed to fix the batteries. James, the mechanic, wanted to check this other factor. They went out to go do that, and while they were out doing that, I'd taken the emergency brake off once to start to leave, and then saw we weren't going anywhere, and put it back on again, and then we began to try to roll it backwards, and decided not to, and I'd taken the brake off again. Each time you put the brake on and off again, you lose a little air, and the pressure went down from like a hundred and twenty to a hundred.

Also, getting it into reverse was a trip. Somebody had to get out and help get it in reverse, because the reverse solenoid was not working. So the brake is not on the emergency brake, and is being held on the foot brake, and every time you put the foot brake on and off, it lets a little air out.

So I told Louise,

"Hold the foot brake down. Don't let any air out of the system. I have to go back and tell them we only have enough air to get the brakes off once, and if we can't do it electrically, we got this way." I went back and couldn't quite make connections, and Louise's leg got tired and just couldn't hold it any more, and *pssst, pssst,* . . .

Do you dig the complicatedness and numbers of different factors and different people cooperating that it took to bring that off? Albert had to do the right thing, I had to do the right thing, James had to do the right thing, and Louise had to do the right thing. Every one of us had to do our part perfectly, or we would never have gotten stuck there. It was complicated, like a *Mission: Impossible!* maneuver—every factor came at exactly the split second timing it took to bring that off.

If you look at where the world is at now, and where the world was at twenty-five years ago, it is clear that twenty-five years ago, we couldn't have gotten off. We would have a harder time getting a thing like this off again right now. There was a period where, for a few years, things were malleable enough that something like this could happen. Infinitely more complex than what it took to stop the bus on the freeway. World War II and the baby boom and Einstein and Tim Leary. And Sandoz and the American Indians, veterans back from the war, Korean War, Viet Nam War, second generation veterans, shaky government. A whole bunch of factors came about to bring this thing off.

But this idea is always latent in mankind, to want to get off and do this thing, and the idea got out.

And it got so wild, and so weird, that something new could happen. And what a profound blessing, that it did. As we get farther from the moment of that birth, we can see that it was a miraculous birth, a renaissance. Those who were in it are responsible, and it's not that that sort of thing is going to happen again and again and again in our lifetime. It's more like that was our chance. So far, we have seized it.

If you go and look around the country, you can see the folks who didn't know it was a chance, or thought it was a fad or a style. But that's not true. It's like remembering where you're at. We're all really One, and we're all really synchronous with all the other people in the world. They are all co-existing with us in this here/now time frame, and this is how we are all doing. Some hungry, some doing pretty good, some overbearing, some taking too much, some not getting enough, but all happening now. And we are as responsible to those hungry people as if they were sitting beside us. That's what Jesus really meant when he said,

"The poor are always with us."—not that you can't do anything about it.

It's a high viewpoint.

Staying high is just to remember that you're high, and not to let yourself be brought down by local, superficial things. It's better for you and for everyone else if you stay on, if you stay high. It's even better for everyone at great distances away, not just up close. So you can't let something up close to you make you put out stuff that everyone else has to take.

You can be by yourself in a meditation room, and be high—and you walk out on the street, and look around and say,

"Oh, look at the trees, look at the nice people on the street."

You walk down the street, like the old hippie prince walking through Golden Gate Park, six inches off the ground—and you come to a corner and you don't pay quite good enough attention, and a car comes, _ssshhhhh_, pretty close,—and you lose a little piece of it.

And you get it back together, and you go on down, and things happen to you. And you try to remember—and then you get downtown and there's stuff going on, cars, noise, get-out-of-the-way, and you're trying to say,

"I'm really stoned. I'm really stoned in spite of all this stuff going on around here. I am still stoned." If you can remember it.

And somebody does something to you that you just can't take, and you get mad, and you lose it, and you can forget that you had it. And maybe months or years later, if you're lucky, you'll say,

"I was stoned. I knew where it was at. I was high with the world. I thought it was okay."

Yet there is something you can do. It's not that it's not all perfect. It _is_ all perfect. But it's a moving perfection, and your free will and your ability to move and change in the situation is part of the ongoing perfection. And if you lay back, it ain't perfect, because that perfection includes that you're doing your best.

Buddha's Four Noble Truths break down to that life is

suffering, and in a very technical sense, I agree with him—in the sense that none of us is born without a little grunt. And we're all going to die, and so did our grand-daddies and great-grand-daddies for generations—and all of us is going to, us and our kids, too. If you look at it from that level, you say,

"Well, life is sorrow. It's inextricable from all of those other things, the leavings and comings, the desires and losings, and ..." but that's what makes life, and life is beautiful, and it's worth every minute of it.

. If you get your mind fixed up, you realize that we're all One, and what you ought to be doing is living a clean, inexpensive life, and trying to help out for the sake of all of us. It's like, For Christ's sake, help out. You can look at Christ and Buddha, and you find that both of them were obviously very telepathically mobile. They had their chakras together, and obviously were psychedelic. They did a lot of mind reading and glowing and fancy stuff. But they didn't teach the Tarot. Buddha specifically refused to speak on astrology. They didn't teach all the little disciplines, because of where they were coming from: No matter where you come from, when you get there, we're all One, and are you going to help out or not? They were really universal and great world teachers, because they came from that place of,

"How you treat the least of my brothers, you've done to me."

"Where two or three of you are gathered together, I am there."

It's just that level of it, which has made them so universal and enabled them to speak to hearts for so many thousands of years. And that's the thing that's happening now.

We are now in the stage of the multiplicity of the cultures. And people are multiplying it unnecessarily. They're making brand names. There's a swami named Devananda, out of the line of Vivekananda, and his trip is the Shivananda Yoga Ashram in the Pocono Mountains. He buys a full-page ad in *TIME* to scream on the Maharishi. He says,

"Meditation is meditation is medititation. Transcendental Meditation is like Pepsi-Cola."

He's very hot about putting a brand name on it that way.

And it is done to have a brand name. They talk about *Transcendental* Meditation and *Integral* Yoga. There's meditation, and there's yoga. That's all. Just meditation and just yoga. There ain't no transcendental meditation. There is no integral yoga. That's just a brand name put on to make their lick distinguishable from someone else's lick, so you'll remember who they are, and turn back on to their lick.

That kind of thing is really confused in today's culture. For example, there is Rolfing. Mrs. Rolf was a lady who knew a lot of the same stuff that Wilhelm Reich knew, that the body can get armored-up in various tight muscles, and you can get bent into funny shapes that you're just held into by tight muscles—and that there are rubbings you can do to people that are significant enough that they don't change back from them. And you have to get deep into it to make that happen. You have to understand that there are muscles under the layers under the layers. You have to know what pulls what in which direction. You have to know a little geometry, and a little leverage understanding to do the thing. It's a fine discipline. The only thing wrong with it is that it has a brand name and that it costs money. It's either a medical service or a spiritual teaching. It should be free in either case.

If we can keep this teaching clear, then we can make some difference. But where it really comes back around to is us, as individuals. How well do we treat each other, and how well do we realize this teaching in our everyday life? Being good to somebody is not like an accident. It's a decision that you do of your free will, on purpose, because you want to, and you think it's right, and know it's all right, and you _be good_ to somebody. You might on purpose decide,

"This argument is petty. I'll drop it."

You don't realize this argument is petty and say,

"This argument is petty. Why don't _you_ drop it?" You realize it, and you shut up, and do what it takes to make it better.

There was a bestseller called, _Looking Out For Number One_, which was written by the author of _How to Win Through Intimidation._ That's all about how dog-eat-dog it is. People come on to me sometimes when they figure out that we're really collective, and that we think it's a spiritual discipline. They say,

"Would you want _everybody_ to be that way?" They feel very threatened by a thousand of us being that way, out of this country of a quarter of a billion people. Well, that thing that is frightened by a thousand raggedy-ass hippies out in the middle of the woods, is the thing that holds back the world.

It is important to understand that there is no enemy which holds us back. There is money, which is fossilized laziness. There are people who think they can get a big enough stash of fossilized laziness that they will never have to work again. This is the general tendency of protoplasm to remain at rest unless otherwise pushed. But there is no sinister intelligence behind that, whatsoever.

It's just that when somebody wants a lot of money, they want to fix it up so they will have social security, so they will be safe. But, there ain't no safety. And once you realize there ain't no safety, and you're going to have to make it on your friends, like you always did—when you're old, as now—if you have any, depending on how you lived your life. No amount of money does it.

We've had these teachings. We saw poor old Howard Hughes, with his fingernails growing out three inches long, sitting around not doing anything for so long. He died mainly from diseases of laziness. If he'd been up and hustling . . . if Howard Hughes had been a ditch digger, he'd be alive now. I wonder if he had known that choice for certain when he was about twenty, what he would have done. What would you do? What are you going to do? It comes to that.

There is law, and there is Grace. Grace is best, but Law works good if you happen to be temporarily out of Grace. You can figure out by the rules how to get back again. You have to get yourself on and healthy and clean, and then you have to start on helping other folks, and you get in a state of Grace, and then you can receive Grace.

You can be in a stoned, loving, telepathic place with anybody you deal with, and if you're not being right with anybody, you're not looking at it from a graceful place; you're looking at it from a smaller viewpoint. We try to look from the biggest viewpoint we can, because it's the only one that makes any sense. Anything that looks smaller than the biggest viewpoint looks like, "Nice guys finish last," and, "Might is right,"—and we *know* it ain't that way.

The Empty Knothole

I want to talk about illusion and reality, and Heaven and earth. We've heard a lot of times that this is all just illusion, but one of the earliest things I figured out was, it ain't like this is illusion and something else is reality, or that this is reality and something else is illusion. It's all whatever it is.

Some people keep insisting on the unreality of the illusion. But that statement is being made from the viewpoint of someone who considers himself to be enlightened, to the viewpoint of someone he doesn't consider to be enlightened. Furthermore, what used to be sort of a sharp division that you could draw with the same kind of accuracy as drawing a line between Democrats and Republicans, has been very fuzzied and muddied up these days, but the fact is that hundreds of thousands of us have had religious experiences. And maybe we don't do it all the time, but we have seen a higher ideal, and we have some idea of it.

We think as people who trip, sometimes better than other times, sometimes right in there. Sometimes a little lost, selfish, unforgiving, angry, something. It's the thing about the illusion and reality. The reason you seek the reality is that the illusion is illusion to the viewpoint of your ego. Now, your ego is nothing but a viewpoint. Your ego is not a something. It's an absence. It's almost like a knothole. When you come up to look through a knothole in a fence, that knothole is empty. And if there's anything in that knothole—a knot, spiders' webs, sawdust—the view through the knothole is obscured, and what you see is modified by that. And if your viewpoint is full of anything at all, it colors the universe that you see, and therefore what you see can be said to be illusion. Got that? Isn't that nice? I got some of that from reading a Tibetan book the other day.

So if you could truly make it so your viewpoint was empty, like the knothole, like it should be—free of self-interest, instead of observing everything to see what you can scam. I used to have a viewpoint on the world like that. As I walked down the street, if I saw anything that wasn't nailed down, I estimated how heavy it was and how much was it worth, and whether I should pick it up and take it with me or not.

But if you can keep your viewpoint clean, you can see, instead of illusion, you can see reality. Now we assume that you don't have to force or coerce people into doing what is right, if they have a glimpse of reality. And we think you should strive for a glimpse of reality yourself, in order that you may know what's right. Then you can up and do it, wholeheartedly, from having figured it out for yourself.

People want a glimpse of reality. One way or another, that's what most of us have been looking for. And one way or another, that's what everybody from Uncle Tim to Maharaj-ji all say that they're going to give you—a glimpse of reality. Some of their realities are so funny it's hard to believe. Some of their realities are very real.

If you see someone be hurt who you know and love—or are just acquainted with—and it leaves you just completely unmoved to see that happen, that's an inappropriate response. We're really all One, and we should share the reality of that as much as we can.

If you had a bunch of people who had a firm grasp on reality, the reality that they would create from their agreement would be the Kingdom of God, or Heaven on Earth. Actually, to say Heaven on Earth is redundant or irrelevant, because you can have Heaven on Wolf-359, Mars, Alpha-Centauri, Aldeberon, Betelguese, no matter where it is in the Universe. It's not a space/time question, anyway. It ain't in Ohio, necessarily, any more than in Brooklyn. When I talk about reality, some people think that sounds awfully Oriental to talk about reality, for some reason or another. That's funny. When I say,

"Seek ye reality,"

I mean you're supposed to be a good, open-minded scientist.

You ain't supposed to say,

"Well, I know what's real," without investigating and observing.

Some people say that reality is the bills and the taxes and the stuff like that, and illusion is love, vibes, and stuff like _that_. Well, reality includes love, miracles, telepathy, extra-sensory perception—are all part of reality. Reality is big enough to include that. That's not the division between reality and illusion. The difference between reality and illusion is,

"Is your mind colored so much that you don't really understand what's going on very well because of it?"

They've tried to say those things for all these thousands of years in such good, simple ways, and the good, simple ways become ritualized until they become so encrusted that they hardly mean it any more, and you have to excavate, and peel off layers of what people have thought about it, to try to get down to what it was, and what it is.

And there's the question of,

"Why are we doing this?"

We have to take responsibility for our part of the Universe. God runs the unconscious part of the Universe, and God runs the conscious part of the Universe; and we're some of the conscious part of the Universe. There is a difference between what the Universe will do and what the Universe considers important. And what the Universe considers important may be different than what we thinking creatures who have free will might think about it.

For instance, Life doesn't care whether you and your spouse get along or not. Life only cares that you have a kid. Life doesn't even care if the kid is well-enough nourished to be intelligent, because the genes can pass on perfect even though a generation has been damaged by starvation. This is acceptable to Life. It keeps the species going another few thousand years to work out its karma. But it is not acceptable to us creatures of free will that we should in any way keep anyone's experience of this Universe at a lower level than it could be. In fact, we have a moral obligation to be sure that every one of us has the best experience of this Universe that we can. Those who are strong and healthy and intelligent should use their energies for the benefit of all, because that's what it takes to make it. This is a moral imperative. If one doesn't understand a moral imperative, one has trouble understanding a lot of the things we say.

So we who have free will are the ones who are responsible, because it does make a difference. But not to part of the Universe. And so, the part of the Universe that it does make a difference to, has to do something about it. We are co-responsible for what we find ourselves in.

This is a society right now that is beginning to jell up like Jell-o. We've got to be very clever to don't congeal with it. We've got to be very fluid and very intelligent to not slide into jelling along with it. The reason it's jelling is that there was a period of change where some people knew more about communications than other people. Now everybody knows about communication, and no matter what idea you're putting out into the world, there is somebody putting out the opposite idea, and they may even have more money than you—lots of chances of it. And there are so many contrary teachings going into the mind, with this tremendous critical mass of communication that we now have, that it has a tendency to seize up. People become suspicious. People say,

"Building an image?"

Who's going to be fooled by an image if you tell them you're building an image? They announce that the government is going to spend umpty-ump million dollars convincing the people. All the people heard that announcement. What are they going to say about that? Don't they know somebody's after their head?

The illusion is that, because it takes so long for news to travel around the world, that by the time we hear about anything, it's so far gone that you have to say,

"Well, that was too bad, but what could you do?"

That's the illusion. The reality is that the hungry people are missing breakfast *now*. Or lunch. Or dinner, depending upon what part of the world they're in. They're missing a meal now. And they missed the last one, and they might miss the next one. And most people who are sick from diseases got it from unsanitary conditions, which is straight-out poverty. Sanitation is one thing that money can buy. The people who are sick from unsanitation are sick from straight poverty, and you can't say that the standard of living that is enjoyed in the United States is divorced from the standard of living that is on the other side of the fences in Panama. It's happening right now, right here, in this reality.

The energy shortage has made the cost of petroleum go up, especially for the poor people. It's like an equation, where they're getting a little short of energy in the form of oil, so they're going to make it up by turning up the amount of energy they get off the people. When you talk about the sources of energy on this planet, there's the sun, and there's coal, and there's oil, and uranium—and there's the people. And the coal and the uranium and the oil would still be peacefully sitting down there with the mouldering dinosaurs' bones, if it wasn't for the people. The riches and energy is in the people. And the people are the energy source.

And people are cynical about religion. It's a shame, but it ain't my fault. Well, it is, too, a little bit, because I ain't perfect, and if I could be perfect, it would help. But it's serious. Religion is the thing that is going to do it. It ain't going to be the Democrats, it ain't going to be the flying saucer people, and one per cent of the people doing Maharishi's thing only means that Maharishi gets a percentage of everybody's action.

The Farm is Holy. The place is blessed by the efforts of thousands of serious people trying hard and praying hard to make it blessed, and it really is. And we're facing some demons. A demon is a soulless entity that exists only for greed and for itself, and will do anything to anybody to get it. One of the demons we're facing is the hospital system. That is a demon which eats human flesh and extracts blood from the poor. Is that enough of a demon for you? Would you rather have your demons with fangs or with stainless steel covering it?

Dr. Leary, in one of his moments of sanity, pointed out that people in the old days had visions of being done up by tigers and wild animals. These days, he said, they more often have visions of being sucked into a paranoid mental hospital, or being done up by some impersonal machinery. It's basically the same visions, but we don't think of it in the same terms. We aren't scared of tigers with fangs. The only tiger you ever saw was behind one-inch steel bars, and it might as well have been a tame pussy cat for all it mattered to you. But the demons are there, like all the corporations: soulless entities that have policies that decide what they do, instead of human beings deciding it. Company policy.

It's enough to make you be concerned about the fate of the planet. There's an interesting thing called the Manichean heresy in Catholicism. It's the idea that God and the devil are in a combat and the outcome is somehow in doubt. The Catholic Church feels so strongly about that heresy that they just excommunicate you for even thinking that.

A couple of times I had visions of deaths that were coming, and I made my distinctions about how to do that on the first time it happened. I felt there was a death coming, and then I felt like I could almost know who . . . I *could* know. . . . I don't want to know. I don't want to know, because I'm going to do my best, and it would sap my strength if I thought that it wasn't going to make it. I'd rather just go ahead and fight it and lose than have it tell me about it.

We have to hang in there with some hope. There's a lot of hope. All the stuff they call poisons came from the earth. It was somewhere safe before we started messing with it, and it can be somewhere safe again. It'll make it.

Protectors of Life

In October, 1977, the native people, the original residents of much of the world, presented a statement to the rest of the planet at the United Nations building in Geneva. The information they presented had been being gathered for months and months all over two continents, and it was the first time that the original people of this entire hemisphere had ever been represented before the community of nations in all these years. I think they realized that was strong: things happened that had never happened before.

No one has ever been allowed to do any form of demonstration at the United Nations building in Geneva, but the Indians were allowed to march in. Grandfather David, the oldest Hopi at 103, came up with a handful of white cornmeal, sprinkling a little to each of the four winds.

The meeting was four days long. There were thirty-five Indian nations represented, sixty-five countries, and non-governmental organizations. The non-governmental organizations are like privileged lobbyists with the General Assembly of the U.N.

I wept every day in the United Nations building. I was not alone. Many people did. It was a far-out experience for me, because basically I had to keep my mouth shut and stay in the background, because it wasn't my scene. But it was okay, because for the first time at any conference of government or any other body of that kind that I had ever seen, I felt represented. They were speaking for me.

There used to be twelve million Indians in the United States, and there's about 800,000 now. There are 20,000 left in Ecuador. Ecuador said they don't have any. One came in and said,

"Oh, yeah. There's still 20,000 of us, man."

They have a different view of birth control than most of the rest of the United States. They ain't interested in it. There was one young married brave, and a bunch of ladies were jiving him about he'd better go home and take care of business. I said,

"I'm sure you can make the sacrifice, can't you?"

And he said, "For my people, man."

There was a good dude named Mr. Chandra from India who was a chairman of one of the plenary sessions. At first, he was so well necktied and white-shirted that I wasn't sure if I was going to trust him or not. But as it got farther along into the thing I began to remember that at one time India was a British colony, and you could tell that from his attitude. He said he had learned three words from the native people. One of them was the idea of a nation, as the Indians presented themselves: a nation, which happens to be scattered across a whole bunch of other people's political boundaries and countries. Another word was sovereignty: there was a way in which they had never yielded sovereignty over themselves to the United States. The last word was genocide. Like our social worker government arm works on the reservations and says,

"Oh, these people are poor. That must be because they're having too many kids."

So they're putting a lot of birth control on them, including a lot of sterilization, and there's only 800,000 of them left. And the Indians are saying,

"Whoa, already. Wait a minute!"

When the Six Nations Confederacy talks about nine million acres of upper New York State, they're not saying that they ought to get all that and all its development and all those towns and all that. They're just pointing out that those nine million acres are the land that they never gave up by any treaties or anything of their own free will. It was just taken, and they would like to work out some negotiations about that, inasmuch as their lifestyle requires a certain amount of territory, and they don't want to give up their lifestyle. They don't want to. Why should they have to?

They were pleading for their existence before the community of nations. And on one end, it was kind of funny. They weren't asking much. They don't use the land up too badly. A bunch of

Indians on the land usually maintain it. It's kind of safe for them to have it. And the other end of it is that half of the untapped energy resources in the United States lies on Indian reservation land. The government has published—not even secret, but published—Department of the Interior plans about how they plan to use all those energy resources; and they have not as yet negotiated with any of the Indians about it.

In the legal session, the Indians spoke about sovereignty, and about nations, and about that they wanted the right to administer the law to their own people in their own way. They pointed out that they had never given up their old ways, and they had never taken citizenship in this country. It had been put on them by an Act of Congress in 1924, and they had never wanted it, and have always fought it. They don't claim to be citizens of the United States, and they came back into the United States on Six-Nations Confederacy passports issued by the elders. They refused to sign any documents that implied that they had citizenship of this country. When we came back in, there were two lines into Customs. One of them said Americans, and the other one said Foreigners. They took the one that said Foreigners. They would not admit to being Americans. No way, by any gesture or implication, would they let anybody say that.

On one hand, these people came with stuff around their neck proclaiming that they were from the Badger Clan or the Beaver Clan or the Snake Clan—one of the traditional clans, and that they were representing not only all these different Indian folks in the tribes, but all the people from the Western hemisphere and the black people under apartheid in South Africa, people like in New Hebrides who have lost their entire island—5,000 Europeans in all the New Hebrides and the 80,000 original inhabitants on a small reservation. They represented all those people, and more. I saw that, by their feathers and their antlers in their costumes and headdresses, and in their prayers, where their blessings were always extended to include the two-legged ones, the four-legged ones, the winged ones, the ones that swim, and those with roots.

They had a viewpoint that was devastating. They said things like, they calculated that Western civilization had gone wrong about 3,500 years ago when people had begun to breed animals so that the decision of how many men there were was put in the hands of people, rather than in the hands of how the animals thrived that season, which was in the hands of God. That was one of the first mistakes.

Then, they said, the Greeks began the practice of building cities, which they referred to by the word, "civilization." That was their viewpoint. It was wild. And it was like they were sitting in judgment.

It was far out to see these people coming down the street in Geneva with antlers, and eagle feathers. If you never saw a live Indian on the hoof, you may not realize that a lot of those headdresses are designed so that they fly as you walk.

Of course, a French-trained *maitre d'hotel* is not to be thought to be a hick by anyone from anywhere, and he was very polite when he asked Phillip Deere if he wanted him to hang up his blanket for him. And there was something that happened that was so obvious in a funny way of a cultural thing. In Europe, when you get trout in a restaurant, they leave the heads on, because they are so civilized that it emphasizes the barbarity of it a little bit. It's a little decadent touch which the Indians, although they are not vegetarians in any sense, felt was so barbaric that they just hooted and laughed and hollered in this fancy restaurant. They said,

"Look. He's got his eyes open. He's looking at me. His mouth's open. Look at him!"

And the polite barbarity of that ancient and decadent European civilization was very apparent.

The Six Nations came in claiming incredible position on the United States and the United Nations. They came in and said,

"We are cultural, spiritual and political continuity with the Six Nations Confederacy that Benjamin Franklin visited previous to the writing of the United States Constitution."

They pointed out that they had a representative form of government when the white man came to the shore, all of whom were representing monarchies—that they were an older civilization. And they did not consider themselves to be underdeveloped. They lived in a relationship with the Universe, they were part of the action. Chief Oren Lyon, of the Onondaga Nation, explained to the United Nations that animals are absolute, they live in a state of grace, they can do no wrong, only we can do wrong. They spoke of recognizing all the cultures of man as part of God's great pattern, yet remaining to their ways that the pattern might remain complete.

There were a few young braves with gear like a shield and crossed spears on the back, but basically one thing struck me about their presentation, across the board. From the Andes and Bolivia and with full feather headdresses all the way down their backs, from Canada talking about the pipeline coming across their reservation, _they were very polite, and they were very forgiving, and they were very gentle in their petition before the community of man, considering what had been done to them and what was still happening._ They talked about things ranging from being considered wards of the government of the United States to being hunted like antelope in the jungles of South America.

A bunch of Indians from Bolivia were there, protesting,

"Please don't take the 250,000 white Rhodesians from white Rhodesia and bring them to Bolivia. The Indians just couldn't hack it."

It was about the demons. It was about the multinational corporations and the economic sector. The simplest, humblest, most natural people in the world went and talked about the multinational corporations and about how corporations owe no allegiance to any culture, society or state of morals whatever, and they move in on indigenous peoples all over the world and rip them off their land, rip them off their labor, rip them off their lives. Rip them off their civilization, rip them off their religion, without anyone being able to say anything about it.

Mr. Chandra pointed out that we NGO's have no real power in the United Nations. We must shout to make our voices heard, for the indigenous peoples of the world. They were really representing the ones with roots and the winged ones and the four-footed ones.

Right now, the most important thing is that there be some naturals left, that there be some traditional peoples left, so we don't all just become created out of television and advertising agencies, becoming two-dimensional people, and not very real.

It's very important that we keep our naturals together. That's why we have a necessity to reach out to the tribal peoples all over the world, and help them survive.

In Geneva, there was a real and personal and true danger to the

South American delegates. They could lose their lives for going to that convention and speaking out about what was happening in their countries. Forgive me for bringing visions of this kind to mind, but I just have to say what it's like for our brothers.

It was like an indictment of civilization. Now, I used to sit around and drink beer and talk jive, but it's really not unreasonable to say this civilization has gone wrong. It's obvious that it's gone wrong, and the native people are trying to get back from it.

Phillip Deere, a Muskogee medicine man, said he goes around and talks to white folks at colleges all the time, but that's almost the only folks interested enough to give him expense money to travel with, and he feels bad about doing it that way. He'd rather be home with young Indians teaching them how to be Indians so they'll keep on being Indians, because if somebody who knows doesn't teach it, they won't keep on.

Phillip Deere also said,

"With all the money the government's spent on the Indians, they haven't made a white man out of me."

The Indian bureau says that they'll probably have all the Indians well enough assimilated to be able to close out having any Indian affairs office in the next ten years or so. The Indians were over in the U.N. saying,

"Ethnocide."

Ethnocide—wiping out a culture—is wrong as genocide.

What do you mean, assimilate?

"What do you mean *we*, white man?" as Tonto said.

They came marching in to the United Nations, with Grandfather David at 103 years old in the front. He was supported by Phillip Deere on one side, and by Leon Shenandoah on the other. Leon is the Todadaho of the Six Nations, and carries a walking stick with all the history of the formation of the Six Nations Confederacy engraved on it. Then came a whole row of chiefs across the front, in fancy headdresses and eagle feathers, flapping a little as they walked. They kept stopping every little while, and gave a little blessing to the ground. As this went on, all the work stopped in the U.N., and all the windows filled up with people hanging out of them looking at this *thing* coming in. It was very strong. They were representing us, and the trees and the birds, for real.

They were the real people. That's what Chief Oren Lyon said,

"We are the real people. We are the protectors of life as it was entrusted to us by our Creator."

I'm so grateful I got to go to that meeting.

I was there in various capacities. I masqueraded as press part-time, and ran around with a couple of shoulder strap camera bags and parked in the press parking lot, and ran through the press entrance and carried cameras around my neck and a tape recorder. And sometimes I would go up to somebody who was wearing a suit, and reveal myself and say,

"I am an N.G.O."

And they'd say, "You are?"

But of all the N.G.O.'s represented, we were the only hippie N.G.O. And part of the time, I just felt like I represented our tribe. I think that's what we are, one of the tribes.

The Indians have a level of civilization that's geared to the culture of a group of people who evolved it; and then they're geared to another level by being keyed to nature. You can be in the west coast, where they carve totem poles, or in the mountains of

Traditional Indian Elders Approach United Nations

New Mexico, or in upstate New York, and if you're a member of the Deer Clan—within each tribe: Mohawk, Seneca, Cayuga, Onondaga,Oneida,there are clans: the Deer clan, the Bear clan, the Wolf clan. And the people who are in those clans, if they run into somebody from another part of the country, they can be like clan brothers with folks who are in that clan in other tribes. They say,

"Oh, Beaver Clan. We've got a few Beaver Clan folks up where we live."

It makes them have a kind of natural organization. It's very far out to be keyed to something natural.

We even made one up. One of the Indians had a weird sense of humor, and would put people on outrageously, to the point where I said,

"This dude must be from the Jive tribe."

One of his friends, who knew him well, said,

"Turkey clan."

They had a strong enough solidarity among them that they could lay a pretty heavy level of jive down on each other. They could say things like that and he wasn't going to quit being an Indian and bug out over it or anything. They were very open and free, and had good vibes. They like to have good vibes, and people did things to try to straighten things that went down that were not cool. I saw people actually stand up and grab hold of a meeting and try to make some sense of it and bring it to focus.

I saw Phillip Deere do that. It was very good. They were having a little controversy, about respect for an elder. Some of the folks were going to overlook this one man bcause they thought he hung out with too many white ladies, and they were about to be a hassle about that. Phillip got up and started talking. He didn't jump off on that subject right away, but he just started talking. It was disorderly, and there was somebody a little drunk on wine in the back corner, and telling loud jokes in Spanish, and a few people in the other corner jiving and not paying attention, and he just started rapping. And some people started paying attention. He seemed very forceful in what he was doing, only they weren't quite following. He was talking about generalities like how he's been studying this Indian question for some years now, stuff like that, generally integrating it, and more and more people beginning to pay attention, and the mind beginning to come together a bit. Then it got to a point where some of the people who were doing their own conversations were resisting and not coming on to what he was saying. And he said,

"I bet some of these folks would like to turn me off like I was a radio, but you can't do that. It's not that I've talked for a long time, but I've hardly begun yet. I intend to talk for a while more, until I get done."

And people began shutting up and paying attention, because they realized that he was implacable, and he was not going to give up until he got the attention.

Then he kept on rapping and kept on rapping until he got them all together, and then he started talking to them about the question of respect for this elder, and whipped it on them about that for a while. He said you may always have a political leader, and you may always be able to find a lawyer, but you may not always be able to find a spiritual leader. He told them about that, and brought the room together. I watched him, and I knew he was a real chief, because he ran meetings, and I could see it was his craft, to run a meeting.

To give you an idea of their basic attitude, I told them a few things about how we do radio communication, and they began to catch on how they could be connected, and I said,

"We could help you guys out with radio. You wouldn't have any trouble getting a license at all."

And they said,

"We ain't gonna get a license."

I really admire their attitude.

It was also kind of funny to watch the U.S. State Department work out when it doesn't think anybody's looking. The government got wind that they had gone out without U.S. passports, and that the thirty delegates from the Six Nations did not have U.S. passports, and were planning on coming back in without U.S. passports, but with passports issued by the elders.

As soon as the State Department heard about that over in Switzerland, they contacted this Indian fellow they knew, and they asked him to go over and tell the chiefs, would the chiefs come around and talk this question over?

Well, it ruined that fellow's reputation with the Indians to even deliver that message. They said,

"If the Ambassador or anybody who is around would like to send a formal letter to our chief, we would accept the communication."

They were chiefs of a nation. You don't send your brother-in-law around to ask them to drop around sometime. They were chiefs of a nation. Send your heavyweight over, and send something on paper that we can refer to later. In a court of law if necessary.

So they kept pushing at that level with the State Department, and the State Department says,

"Well, if everybody will just come over here, we'll let you back in the U.S., if you just fill out this form, and it costs $25 apiece to fill out the form." The form, it turns out, is an application for a passport. They just said,

"No way. We ain't doing any of that."

So they were working it out. The State Department was trying to figure it out over in Switzerland, so there wouldn't be any embarrassment when they got back to the States. So you can see what that's about.

I saw another example of that. The *International Herald-Tribune* said the United States was denied access to this meeting. They reported that the U.S. had received charges of genocide from a meeting which would not allow the United States to come in and make its statement. But I happened to be present when the chair recognized the delegation from the United States and was told they hadn't arrived yet, can you wait for a while? And then we waited another fifteen minutes or so and the chair recognized them again, and asked if they were there. And they weren't there, or ready to talk or something, and then we waited for a while longer, and finally went on with the proceedings. In fact, it held up the proceedings for half an hour to forty-five minutes trying to get it together for the American delegation to talk. It used up the time that had been allotted for Grandfather David Monongye of the Hopi to deliver the Hopi prophecy. He didn't get to do that, while we waited around for the Americans to show.

Well, I don't think that Cyrus Vance and Jimmy Carter are figuring out a cheap-ass lie like that. That's some low-level flunky over there who's trying to contain it in a small country so it doesn't get out, trying to keep what's really going on from getting out in the world community.

Anyway, they got back to the United States, and they hadn't compromised about anything. I had to part company with them at the line where it says, "U.S. Citizens," because I had to cop to having been a U.S. citizen. Which was sort of a funny thing to have to do in front of them, but there I was.

The government gave them a lot of forms to fill out. The chiefs had gotten together on the airplane before we landed, and said, "Don't fill out this blank which implies you're a citizen," and "In this blank, put in your Indian name, not any other names."

So they went ahead and filled them out, as they would from their nation, in their way—and then refused to sign them, because it would imply some consent to anything the government might be putting up. So they wouldn't sign the forms, and they actually did not have any documentation other than their own passports. What the government did was to make as little fuss about it as possible, to try not to underline it too much. But they _did_ come back in that way.

The press in various countries treated it in various ways, according to how they felt about it. Some countries didn't admit that it went on. The heavies were all there taking pictures of it, and they've all got footage of it. I think they are laying back to see if it gets any heavier play anywhere, and the rest of them will come up with it. We saw CBS and UPI and all those people there.

One thing that was funny was the question of accents. At one point, the interpreters were going to quit. They had never heard so much Spanish pronounced in so many weird dialects, and French pronounced in so many weird Indian dialect fashions, because the folks from South America and Canada were all speaking Spanish and French with definite accents from this hemisphere. The interpreters were speaking Spanish out of Barcelona and French out of Paris, and were not used to them weird Indian accents. It was fun to work out that stuff.

The Indians feel like they have a system working. They feel like they have a contract with God, with the animals, with the trees, to coexist with them in a non-destructive relationship. Sometimes they eat meat; and I can't quibble with them about that question. They may have that relationship with this continent, because they live on this continent and are native to this continent. They are part of the rock and bone and chemical and blood and soil of this continent, and whatever relationship they made with God is a relationship they made. But we who come onto this continent in the tracks of the *conquistadores* and oppressors should remember that, although we are not in agreement with the crimes of our grandfathers, the sins of the grandfathers are carried on to the third generation. We do have a responsibility. On the Farm, we are living on five civilized tribes' land. It would be theirs had it not been for our ancestors taking it away from them. I don't believe we have the same contract with the continent that they do. We should be vegetarians and take as little as possible, considering there's so many of us.

Tribes foster diversity, because that is what they are—little cultural pockets. As long as they're coming out of "We are all One," as long as they're coming out of God's universal pattern, as long as they're coming from the idea that everyone has to be represented, I can't hassle them about the details.

They had a peace pipe, and they said it was made of red stone, the color of the earth and the color of the red man. I had a peace pipe bowl at home. It was green, for the color of what I smoked in it. Different tribes have different ways.

Somebody got a little hot that the Indians lived collectively, and said something about communists or something like that. The Indians said,

"We did not invent *either* the Catholic Church *or* Marxism."

I guess one of the things that happened to me at that meeting was that I felt some of the most peyote I've ever felt in my life without having eaten any. I saw old chiefs and old medicine men get up and say things that were so true that it made my hair stand on end. I broke out in goose bumps and cried on the spot several times—and looked around and saw Europeans in suits and neckties also leaking. Pressmen were visibly affected, and you know how they are. It was very strong.

The Magic of Forgiveness

The situation today is almost exactly parallel to that of the people in the time of Jesus. There was an old way of thinking and a new way of thinking, and the new way has a certain freedom, which the old way might have had when it was new. Jesus said you can't put new wine in old bottles. You can't force new thoughts into old forms. You have to let them go into their own form, and then see what they're like. He also said that the Mosaic code was a set of law that, if you followed all of this law you would be all right—you wouldn't make any mistakes; it'd be pretty good. The difference between that and what was supposed to be brought by a Messiah like Jesus was that there is grace and forgiveness. You can be forgiven. You can be absolved. You can start with a clean slate.

That was revolutionary. Now we find ourselves in a similar kind of condition, where the old order is Freud and behaviorism, the old order of psychology, the old way of looking at the mind. It is a way of looking at the mind that this culture put together. But there is a new way of looking at the mind, as being created eternally in the here-and-now, rather than a long string of karma leading back to something that you can't do anything about anyway, because it's in the past. A lot of the people who have the hardest times, whom I would really like to help the most, are running their minds and their lives out of an old psychological model where you make a mistake and you correct for it, and that puts you in another position, and you correct from that into another position, and each one of these mistakes gets you so attached and blows your mind so bad that it dims your memory of your original position. Every time you correct and move to a new position because of something that you did, trying to get better, you get in the position of the gambler who goes up and puts down a dollar and loses it, and says,

"I'll get that back," and puts down two dollars, because if he wins on that $2, he'll make up that dollar he lost, too—and loses that, and he puts down four dollars and loses that. Eight dollars, and loses that. And sixteen, thirty-two, sixty-four dollars, $128, $256, $512, $1,096, bang, bang, bang, losing fast, getting in, rent money, next month's car payment, school loan, down the tubes ... can't lose that dollar, gotta double up. Your attachment to not losing that dollar meets up with the laws of geometry and math and you find yourself owing more money than there is in the Universe on your next bet, in order to break even, and you keep losing the dollar you started with. That huge astronomical sum of money can get you very uptight, and it forces you into a position that you really hadn't intended when you started.

That's like having made a mistake, and noticed by the expression on people's faces, which is so telepathic and easy to read, that once again you've been a turkey. And you say,

"Oh. Did it again. All right, this time I'll really blow their minds. This time I'll really make them think I'm their true brother, man. I'll blow their minds." And you go out and bet that $4,963,112, one more time.

It's also like the kind of model of thinking that says if you be something you didn't like, that you're going to have to be in debt somehow about it: if you offended yourself, that you're in debt. Offending other people is one thing. Offending yourself is another. There's this chain that seems like a steel chain around you, because if you make a mistake and it changes you, and you make another mistake and you try to do better, how do you get out of it? The only way is through a piece of magic, like forgiveness and redemption. Even if you did bet your way back out of that hole you were in, it's such a bad practice that it wouldn't teach you anything, and the next time something came up, you'd find yourself in the same place again, and still be a gambler. So even if you won that way, you'd lose anyway.

What you have to do is to somehow nullify the whole game. You have to step outside of the entire structure of it. You can't be in that any more. You can't be involved with winning and losing. It can't be about praise and blame. You'll drive yourself nutty if you try to catch up that way, because nobody will blame you harder than yourself. The kind of blame you put on yourself will hurt you. We all make mistakes.

Magic and forgiveness are very interesting tools. You don't do a piece of magic to magic yourself cool. You can use the piece of magic to magic yourself unattached so someone else can get cool. So you can forgive them instantly. In that little book by Father Juan Mateos, he said one of the criteria of the true community is that forgiveness is speedy and sure. Not only are you forgiven, but it doesn't leave you hanging around being paranoid for a long time worrying about it. For the sake of the love and the sanity in the community, it's a magical use of forgiveness. What happens in a meditation is not that you figure out if you did wrong, but that you go to a different place and you be redeemed. You be made whole. Healed. Your blackboard gets erased, and you come out not having forgotten that you did something dumb—never that, it's useful to know you did something dumb. It's how you grow. You ain't gonna do _that_ again!

And the very fact that redemption can happen, that you can be healed and cleansed regardless of what dumb thing you did, is grace. It says in the Secret Oral Teachings or the Precepts of the Gurus,

"For he who understands the unsulliable nature of the intellect, there is no need to seek absolution for past sins."

If you know that you cannot dirty the mind, no matter what you think, this is to understand true forgiveness. It's not the forgiveness of man, which moves on a whim or on a liking, but the forgiveness of God, which forgives on an eternal law, and is fair for all. It is not administered by man. That is to understand that there is Grace.

The criteria you should use about checking out a religion should be much, much harsher than those you would use checking out a car or a piece of land that's going to indebt you for a hundred years. You should have really high standards, and that is a context in which a teaching appears.

As I've said a lot of times, I love the Moonies, Hare Krishnas, their students, as people. But I have some things to say about those teachers. This is a generation that has grown their hair and turned religious. Who in the world could have thought such an outrageous thing would happen? This is truly inscrutable Providence, is it not? What a weird idea. Mind boggling, in fact. Hard to understand, but apparently nonetheless dragging on all these years. Apparently quite true.

There were people who came from all over the world because of the energy that was manifested in this country. Some of them came out of a true concern for these young people who were obviously led into levels of religious thought that tested your soul, your mind, your sanity. Some of them came from all far corners of the world to come to help out. And some of them came because that was where the action was. Like when you cruise down the Strip, you look for the drive-in with the most action in it. A lot of them came here for the action.

Now I have said stuff about one teacher or another, and the main reason that I try to avoid it is just that the vibrations of that frame of head produces kind of a hassle, and you shouldn't run people's heads through that kind of vibrations unless there's a good reason. But some of the teachers that came here were hitch-hiking on the energy of this generation, and they should be grateful to be in this incredibly heavy juice. For them to come here and claim to be the King of the Universe like Fat Boy did, on stickers you'd glue to mailboxes which stay on for months and months, is an affront to the psychedelic sensibilities of a generation who have learned a better yoga than that and a better truth than that.

I make a very strong distinction there, and it's like this. I think that as a citizen of the United States, and as little as possible one of the taxpayers of the U.S., that I have an obligation that the government runs fair, according to the principles of the Constitution. According to that, I would say the government should make no law respecting the establishment of any religion. Like it said back in the Constitution very plainly, a person should be free to follow whatever religion they care to follow. If it means that their magic ritual is to curdle themselves in soy butter, I would defend their right to do that, and I would maintain that the government should make no law about that. As long as they're not harming anyone else by their practices, they should be allowed to do that. One of the Holiest things about this country is that we allow that freedom.

Also, under the First Amendment, we have freedom of speech. As a human being, rather than a member of the government, but as an individual with no police power to enforce my opinion, and nothing but a sharp eye and a big mouth, I reserve the right to say whatever I see all the time about anybody, no matter what the subject matter is, or the company, forever.

So I would say when the government got down on Scientology, I was with Scientology—although I haven't liked Hubbard's act since 1950. But when it comes to the government against Scientology, or even the government against Moon . . . although, I have to say that I was disappointed that Moon played so fast and loose with the money as to bring down the feds on the entire non-profit structure. That was just evidence of being a buccaneer, as far as I'm concerned, a freebooter.

But the thing about forgiving is that if you forgive, you don't have to forget. Because then it is filed properly with nothing extra laid on it. It's just this information in your regular sane memory like anything else, without any red flags on it, so you don't really have to forget. It just goes to an appropriate level of memory.

That thing that was alive in Germany in World War II lives now, and it must be resisted, not in the sense of resisting evil, but in the sense of not just turning things loose on the people that are hard on them. And if something is coming out of a premise that people are just to be slaughtered like cattle, or used in that kind of a fashion, you can't allow a falsity like that to go down. You have to call it like you see it every time you see it, and you have to not be afraid. Some of these people who give testimony about things that happened twenty-five years ago are just as much in danger of their lives for testifying today as if they'd given it twenty-five years ago. Because that thing lives. There's a little of it in South Africa, right now.

And we have responsibility. I just pray and pray that we can steer through these next few years without being put into another big world war. It's just so dangerous for mankind right now. But you have to not be intimidated, and you have to be courageous, and you have to say what went down, for the sake of other people if not for yourself.

Any time anybody shows any compassion—man, woman or child, or other critter—that's some of God's grace. That there is compassion at all is God's grace. That we understand compassion shows that there's such a thing as God's grace. Compassion has a technical electrical sense, and a philosophical sense. The philosophical sense is kind of like empathy and sympathy and understanding and all that kind of thing, but the technical sense of it is that we are telepathic. Whether or not we believe in that word, we understand it. It doesn't make any difference. We're telepathic, not like Dr.-Watson-come-here-I've-invented-the-telephone, or something like that. You're telepathic: we all breathe the same air and live out of the same chemicals of the same earth, and our minds partake of a lot of the same territory all the time.

Our bodies and telepathy move in several levels. Compassion is one of the forms of telepathy. It's body telepathy, where you feel what other people feel.

But just as people perceiving the same thing and understanding the same thing about the same time, minds be exactly in the same place at the same time, there is also a phrase that people use, "hurts your feelings." What does that mean, "Hurt your feelings." What do feelings mean?

Feel-ings. Feels that go on. You must feel them, because they're called feelings. Now where do you feel? You're not being touched. You're just feeling something, and your feelings hurt, or get hurt. I had an example the other night that was very clear. My kid, Sam, had been hanging out in my room for a long time and we'd been pretty happy together, and it got to be a little hassle just at the last minute. So when he said,

"I'm gonna go in the other room,"

I said, sort of sharp and thoughtless,

"Good."

And he said,

"Awwwww."

It was a little uncompassionate to drop that on him like that. I had to go back and get straight about it. So I said,

"I'm sorry. And we had a good time hanging out with you."

And it was better.

Into the Juice

I've been to a few freelance places lately, places where it was up for grabs, where they were working it out on the spot about how it was going to happen. Those big demonstrations like Seabrook and Diablo Canyon and Rocky Flats are places where a lot of working it out goes on, and it kind of reminded me of old times on Haight Street to be mixing it up with a bunch of folks like that. There is a recurrent thread that has been going through, under the rough general theme of Into the Juice, and Other Psychic Phenomena.

It's one of those things that people dread hearing about themselves,

"Oh, no, not me, never touch the stuff," but secretly knowing, "Yeah, yeah. Into the juice."

One of the first things that is almost axiomatic is that if someone is truly into the juice and you're trying to tell them about it, they will be able to ignore everything you say. Some people affect not to understand what is meant by *into it*. It means having a real fondness and liking and attachment, when you're really into it. It's one thing to be knowledgeable about it like somebody who is really into electronics or something, and has been studying it or working on it or something like that; but somebody's who's into the juice is deep into it.

Then why do you say, *the* juice, into *the* juice?

It's the ambient energy which we are all sharing; and it doesn't benefit us in any way to think of it as your juice or my juice. What we really need is to be fair about how it works. So it's *the* juice.

Why is it the *juice?* If you get into an orange, you get into the rind and the rind is a container. Then, under the rind there's the white part, and it's kind of pulpy, like packing and container, and then inside that is another little thin bag, almost like saran wrap, a little bag in a little wedge-shaped slice. The little bag is another container, so you haven't truly got to orange yet. You're just working on container through all that stuff so far. And then you crack open the next level and there's a bunch of little bitty slender, fibrous envelopes that are full of *juice*. Which turns out to be the where-it's-at-ness of the orange, after all, of the very orange itself.

It's like the juice of life. And it was spoken very well by Dylan Thomas in his poem about the Savior when he said,

Rarer than radium and commoner than water.

This is the thing that learned men spend decades on, give up hopes of family and immortality and children and take Holy Orders and study for the rest of their life in hopes of obtaining a glimpse of it. But no baby that is born lives without it. And it is present where life is present.

In another poem, Dylan Thomas is talking about a vine growing and those tendrils reaching out and curling around things, and he says,

The force that through the green fuse drives the flower
Drives my green age;

The thing about being into the juice is it's really one of those broad-spectrum things that describes a multitude of human frailties. For example, if you meet somebody and you say,

"How you doin'?" and they habitually say,

"Well, . . . pretty good," and there they are in front of you, healthy, skin's pretty good, eyes pretty good—they're obviously not sick or anything. Everything's obviously pretty good, pretty fair shape, but they won't just say,

"All right."

That's important, to let somebody know it's all right. When you walk down the street in a big city, and the people pass so many people, the greetings can get worn thin from usage. And the people say the barest minimum when they see one another, to pass by through so many people. One guy will walk past another and he'll say,

"Aaay," and the other will say,

"All right!"—to let everybody know you're okay, if you are.

The thing that made everybody get tired of Richard Nixon was when it really became evident that he was into the juice: that he was into it for the money and the glory, which for him was into it for the juice.

It is easier to understand a lot of behavior if you really understand the energy and how completely necessary it is for everyone to have it—just like oxygen, just like water. Got to have it, got to have it, got to have it to make it. If you run too long without it, you start getting sick and crazy. There are a lot of folks whose level of consciousness between sanity and not is purely a matter of the energy; and if they can survive in a high energy situation, they can be well and healed. If they can be in a high energy situation and recognize that the ambient energy—all around us and inbetween us, like the air, like the space—the ambient energy really belongs to everyone. And it is legitimate to say, "Help!" and ask for a focussing of that energy.

The advent of big time energy into this country back about ten, fifteen years ago, made it suddenly get very heavy juicy all over. And it also got very heavy to see who could stand to be in a high energy environment. Otherwise nice, ordinary, sane people who you would think were just the nicest folks, found themselves deep into the juice, climbing the sound towers, taking off their clothes at rock concerts, deep into it.

People can be so much into the juice as to go into contra-survival behavior. Being really strung out on juice is much like being a speed freak. And it works in the same way, because the thing with any of the speeds—benzedrine, methedrine, dexadrine, or whatever you ever heard of that was speed, caffeine, whatnot—is that they give you the illusion of energy. The reason they give you the illusion of energy is because it's actually taking some of your tail and feeding it to you. So it really is the illusion of energy. It's burning up some of you, but the methedrine or the caffeine or whatever has no calories in it, no vitamins, no minerals, no nothing. It doesn't have any food value; it does not replace or give any energy to you. It merely is a chemical exciter that excites your body into giving up some of its reserves of energy. This creates the illusion of energy. And obviously if you run on that kind of energy and don't eat, then you're just going to be burning your old thing, until you get to how we used to see the classic speed freaks on the streets, skinny and grey and burned out.

But if you're deep into the energy, you can get so far into the energy that you don't eat. You have plenty of energy on even though you may be hungry and need food, if you can take all the attention from the surrounding people and keep yourself buzzed on energy, you won't really feel such a necessity to eat. And you would rather even take it in that vibratory medium, and keep yourself buzzed on everybody's energy, and not eat. And your body runs down and you make worse decisions as you get fatigue toxins. This is like a psycho-physiological-chemical-schizophrenic break, right? Into the juice, actually. Just into the juice.

The important things to learn are that there are times when you can live on that kind of juice, and there are times when you can't. If you're going into a time of fasting and prayer and you felt you've decided to do that, and you know how much you can take and you're not going to overdo your body or something, maybe you just live on that for a while. I know there's been many a meal I've passed up because I just wasn't ready to back down to the material plane enough to eat yet.

You're not supposed to just do your bulldozer work and your hauling with that kind of energy. You're not supposed to drag your old electro-chemical robot around from place to place on that kind of energy. You're supposed to eat a nice, balanced diet. Run your reactor, get your good chemical energy chains working. Run your machine on energy that is derived from how you eat. And run your mind, and run your soul, and run your spirit on that other kind of energy. Don't just use it to grind along on the starter motor, but really use that kind of energy to get off with, not just to live and make it with. Sometimes you have to use it to live and make it with. But that should be like emergency, like going on oxygen. But it's rarer than radium and commoner than water.

Decisions about being into the juice are some of the most important decisions that people who are trying to govern themselves can be involved with. We have to be able to understand, in an adult fashion, the difference between being "into the juice" by stepping too far forward, and shirking responsibility by not stepping forward far enough. A fine dividing line.

There was a word which the hippies have used for a while, *astral.* But that word is a hassle, because folks don't know what *astral* means very good. Instead of the astral plane, you could call it the plane of soul communication and people would understand it better. The plane of soul communication, where people's souls can intercommunicate. Souls are not as attached to form as people's bodies are. People's bodies pretty much like to keep on being the same thing; if they look into a mirror and see something different the next day, it freaks them out. But your soul can just amoeba on out there, just stick out a pseudopod— to anywhere. To anywhere, regardless of space and time.

When I'm out tripping around it's frequently so noisy that the synchronicity becomes obscured; but one time at Diablo Canyon it was turned up very high on me. I was standing about a hundred and fifty feet back from the stage, listening to this guy talk. And he was doing a free form poem, which would occasionally go into a chant of some kind—and all of a sudden, right through the middle of this free form poem that he's doing, he says,

"And that great ocean wave is going to wash up to that little sand castle of a nuclear reactor and wash it away in the great tide of human opinion," and stuff like that.

And as he says that, I look down and there's this nuclear sand castle at my feet, about three feet in front of me. Somebody's made a little sand castle like a nuke. And I look at that and we're standing on dry sand. There's a lot of people scattered around us; there ain't been a wave in a long time. It is thick with ten, fifteen feet of people back to where the wet sand starts.

So I look down at that thing and I say, "Wow." And the synchronicity gets a little thicker. When something like that happens, it goes _click!_ and it keys you in a little bit, to the level of it. So I dug that and I grabbed for my camera to take a picture of it and I'm zeroing in on it and focusing, and not even noticing,

when suddenly I'm wet to about the ankles. And the water comes through and is just washing it away while I'm taking a picture of it while he's still talking about it.

Things got very clear and very crystal and very thick

for a minute.

But it takes a heavy trip to make you notice, when there's all that stimuli going on. When I was just back from that trip, I had just got out of a hot bath and was laid out across the bed sweating, and I heard one of the girls say, out in the kitchen,

"Paul, you want a bite?"

And just completely from nowhere in my mind, I said, "Too hot."

Paul says,"Yeah," and puts it in his mouth, and he screams and she says,

"Too hot, eh? Sorry."

And it almost wrecked my nap, because I snapped to attention so hard from where did *that* come from? Just so cleanly and without fuss, a little piece that was intuition. And it was clean enough and separated from the rest of me enough that I could say,

"Oh, that one was intuition. Far out."

As the synchronicity gets thicker and thicker, we are reminded that we are all co-creating this. All the people in the world are co-creating this environment; in every plane and level you can think of—including the giant pollutions from the nuclears and the tankers and the oil things which are changing the environment around us, to the most subtle level of agreement in the minds of mankind.

We live in a time that is very important right now, and this question of the juice is very important right now. Whether or not you believe in and live by the juice makes a lot of difference in what kind of political situation, civil rights, human freedoms and human quality of life you're going to have.

I've been paying close attention to my experiences with the juice for a number of years now, and I've been following it closely to see how it works. It's from the results of those observations—not just those observations, but from those occasional intuitions—that I try to help figure out what's a good karmic path for a little microcosm of society that has an effect a long way out from where we are—how we be affects how everybody be's a little bit.

It is good if somebody takes care of the juice. It helps if everybody does, but it's good if somebody is just paying attention to that. You have to be in shape to do it—like if you go out on the wood crew and you ain't in shape, the next day you're going to be all sore.

The demonstrators at Diablo Canyon were a hastily gathered group of people, so there wasn't any particular common thing among them except that they didn't want to fry. So on the way back out from jail when they were taking us out to the park, the bus driver, a middle-aged lady, gets a call on the CB telling her which park to take us to. Some folks, not CB listeners, didn't hear that. So we went past the first park where there were some people, and immediately this girl in about the third row leaps up and starts shrieking at the driver,

"Are you going to continue to oppress us in this fashion? You're not letting us off by the park!" and just started doing this number to the bus driver.

This girl was in her early twenties, with a more mature hippie lady who turned around and said,

"Sssssshhhh, shut up, you do damage to our movement."

"But she's . . ."

"Down, down," cooled her out and settled her back down. It was a little bit of a tense situation, seventy-five people in a bus about to be released to freedom after having spent the night in jail, but the girl was like a fifteen-amp fuse in a twenty-amp slot, and she went . . . _sssssttt_ and burnt out when so much attention came up.

That's how a lot of folks are. They may be in pretty good shape because they may stay out of heavy situations, but you can't always guarantee that you aren't going to be in a heavy situation ever—and when you talk about the real training of, say, a doctor, a doctor can have all the medical knowledge and all that stuff, and if he hasn't a little presence of mind to make common sense observations and handle the situation developing in front of him, nobody would call him a doctor. The essence of it is to go into a scene, call the situation, figure it out.

Also, with the discussion system at Diablo Canyon, it was hard to tell about individuals being into the juice, because there was a _system_ that was into the juice, as well as some of the people. And there was a bunch of people trying so hard to not be into the juice that they were allowing themselves to be ripped off pretty easily by the folks who _were_ into the juice.

You can find somebody who'd demonstrate against about anything in this country. Folks demonstrate against sassafrass tea. The cops know that, too, so the organizers want everybody to be real nice and don't look to the cops like a bunch of professional demonstration groupies. There are enough demonstration groupies in the U.S., and it's a rich enough country that they can get around well enough that you can about throw something once a month and guarantee a few thousand people for it, no matter what it is. If you're going to make any difference, like in the nuclear movement, you have to surpass that statistic quite a ways so you can attract their attention. But there were folks out there who were saying,

"Five hundred people. With this amount of power we can rule . . . " Those people had a vastly overrated idea of what five hundred people was. When you're working in a country of 240 million people, the government is quite willing, statistically, to write off any particular five hundred people as nuts.

Some people have a hard time with high-juice situations—they just blow out. Blowing out in high-juice situations mostly stems from not keeping yourself in shape in the day-to-day interactions as you go along. If a kid cries, you have a choice between hearing it the first time, jumping up and doing something creative, or hanging out for a while before you do anything about it, until the kid gets a little madder. Suppose you decide,

"I'll lay here a little longer, until the kid gets a little madder."

If you do that a few times, then when you come into a heavy situation . . . those were the exercises that would have got your psychic muscles up so you wouldn't freak out in a heavy situation. Doing the right thing and the courageous thing under pressure is not a question of doing the exceptional thing; it's a question of that you always do what's right. It's not the exceptional thing. So you have to build yourself to be able to do that.

The motivation is another interesting thing at these nuke demonstrations. They divided us up in groups and gave the groups names and emblems. And there were various ceremonies that were for the sake of raising energy, not for the sake of a person or a project, but for the sake of raising energy. It was sort of like cheerleaders. You have cheers, which are group mantras, and you chant the mantras real loud. And if you start to go home, a bunch of people come and tell you you're really needed here, and you ought to do it like this, and you got to stick with it right here.

And if somebody comes and tries to get you out of one of those, it's said that they're from the wrong side, you shouldn't listen to those folks if they're from the wrong side, and all of that.

I think the same techniques they used to run the nuke rally can be found in the way Moon runs a training camp. The difference is motivation. Moon says it's to save the world. Everybody says, "You've got twenty million dollars. We don't believe you."

The anti-nukers say it's to save the world, and people say, "Well, you know, plutonium is nasty stuff. Maybe it's worth the amount of regimentation you're going under in order to have a strong movement to go over the fence with." But it wasn't me who said that last statement. That was an editorial observation.

Now, that's a case of corporate into the juice, on one of those sides, anyway, or organizational into the juice.

The thing about talking to other people is that talk is so cheap, don't get uptight about talk. The best way to be about an argument is just to let go and see what comes down. Oberve the phenomena, take good notes. No sense arguing. It will unfold itself, we'll know.

The people who are really moving people are the people who show a lot of love, like this man from Lawrence Radiation Laboratories, Dr. Gofman. He was speaking out about the nukes. He's a heavy physicist and all, but there's a lot of heavy physicists who have come out against the nukes. But he communicates his fatherliness and his grandfatherliness and his love about it. And he's not coming on angry or anything; he's pointing out that this is going to hurt a lot of people and you've got to come from a compassion and a love place. He never did get into screaming and fist-raising or anything like that, but he had about 15,000 hippies sitting listening to a science class like none of them ever did in college. Really respectfully, and really trying to learn out of a love, heart place, and that's what really has to make the difference.

Juice is life force. I'll tell you a little tale that happened to Michael O'Gorman one time when we were first here on the Farm. His wife, Cara, and her twin sister, Mary, were being midwives, or at least one of them was at that time, and they were out on a call. Michael was driving them, coming up from down on the Farm, and they were coming past the greenhouse going toward the mill. There used to be a stump about two feet high, sitting in the middle of a bunch of weeds about two-and-a-half-feet high, and it was just off to the side of the road. Michael was on a call, and somebody there was slow in the corner, and he decided he would go around them on the outside. He pulled around them on the outside and went into this big old oak stump. He was driving an old Travelall, and it stopped in however long it took the bumper to cave back into the radiator, and bashed both the twins, Cara and Mary, up against the dashboard.

I was on the same call, and came walking into it and found this thing. I stuck my head inside and I turned on this flashlight and both the twins had bashed their foreheads and there was a stream of blood running down their faces on both of them. They were both just realizing at the time I arrived that they weren't seriously hurt—and they were both very relieved, and they were both laughing. So I stuck my head in, and I turned on this flashlight, and here's these identical twin ladies bleeding and laughing. It's quite a funny looking scene. Tremendously energetic—the only thing in the scene that's not energetic is Michael in the driver's seat, feeling deep blame and looking over his shoulder at the bashed up twins.

The energy that was being released there was a special kind at that point, because there was a little relief that they weren't hurt, and there was the life force—direct life force, the bleeding. There was life force being given off by the blood cells which were out of their medium and giving off their life force. The jar and the bruise and the jolt of it had jarred everybody loose from a little bit of life force, and they were a little bit high on it, a little giggly, and it was very pretty and colorful. Even the blood was a little bit pretty and colorful in the vision inside this Travelall, and when I stuck my head in and turned on the flashlight, I realized that this Travelall was full of life force. They had all just been joggled loose from it and it was just drifting away. They were going to be a little shaky and shocky in a few minutes, but not right now; they were high on the energy that was joggled loose. I felt like I had a vision of life force, and that I had just seen it made manifest in that little scene, bubbling like champagne. It was just pretty, exciting.

Now, this was all back a while ago when this went down. At one time, we used to be loggers. We cut a little firewood even yet, or we might clear somebody's land. But at one time we were going to be loggers. We'd been logging for a while, and I hadn't been to the woods, partly because it was a long ways out there and there was so much heavy action on the Farm, but partly because I just had an intuition about it. One day it came to where I sort of had to go to the woods. We'd been logging long enough, had enough people involved, it was an industrial scene, with chain saws and tractors and logging trucks and loaders and a logging truck that loads itself—it picks up an eight-foot oak log and hook-shots itself into itself— it's really thunderous equipment, and they'd been cutting over on the Martin Farm, and they'd cut out a little clearing which they had just opened up in the woods at that point. They'd limbed all these trees—some of them were two feet, two and a half feet thick, and they had limbed all those trees, and the branches were all laying around on the ground. They were loading the logs in the truck, and there were branches and leaves lying around on the ground—shiny leaves the sun was just shining right off of, glinting and glittering. And I had this wild feeling, because at some deep level it looked just like the twins in the seat of the Travelall, at some real deep life-force emotional level. And all those freshly cut branches laying there on the ground were giving up their life force. They weren't dead or anything yet—it would take them days—they were giving up their life force, and it was bubbling off of them like champagne. And it was bright and it was pretty, but I knew what it was. And I saw that even as attractive and as pretty as it was, I wasn't into it much. When I came home from being out in the woods that day, I got sick when I got home. I went sick for about two days. At first, nobody could figure out what might be wrong with me, but I knew what was wrong—what was wrong is that I got sick at just seeing the woods like that, seeing all that life force just going away that way. It wasn't like life force trading to protect life force. It wasn't like building houses for the children—a bunch of it was going for railroad ties. I guess we were building with some of it, but it was just obvious that cutting those hundred year-old, two hundred year-old trees was sort of an unfair life force bargain with the world. It looked that way because that's how stuff works: you see it, you understand it, and it doesn't have to be translated to you. You just look at it, and you see it, and you understand it. We were into the forest's juice.

We talked it over, and we decided that we couldn't do it

anymore. And it was funny telling Homer about it, when we'd been partners in his saw mill. He said,

"How deep does this conviction go with you? I hope we're going to get to use the logs that we already cut; I got more logs than I strictly need."

We explained it to him and he was fine. He loves us and forgives us for being so nutty sometimes, but we gave up that kind of logging, logging for money. We still might clear some land for somebody, something like that, but we ain't gonna be in that business.

The thing about being into the juice is that it's so pretty and so attractive that it's very difficult to stay out of it; everybody wants to get into the juice. And there's ways you can do it: there are skills and crafts of being into the juice.

I saw a girl at the community kitchen one time, and some people had come to eat from maybe the woodshop, and for some reason they were out of their place—they were supposed to stay at the woodshop and have it delivered to them, or something—they didn't do it right, somehow. And this lady got mad at them, and fried out about eight or nine guys that had been working since early morning for not being in the right place in chow line. And I was present, and she didn't really notice I was present, and then noticed later I was, and was sorry she had come on so strong—and then had to think about what was the difference in whether I was there or not, why should that make any difference at all how you should be to people. The thing about that was, she was probably right about the facts of the matter, but those eight or nine guys, had to personally, each one, make an adjustment in his energy for having been confronted in that fashion. Each one of them had to personally decide to overlook this, each one had to personally forgive her for what was going on—and they did. And they tried to get it a little better, to raise it up a little.

Sometimes you see something like that go down. And sometimes the thing is handled perfectly, telepathically. In this case, she realized where she'd been at and didn't want to have been that way, and they didn't want to put it on her, because they were all going to continue living the rest of the day and it might as well be a good one, so everybody overlooked it for the same reason.

She was into their juice. That was like a little hold-up, getting a shot of their energy, putting a little bummer on them.

A lot of people they call crazy are so deeply into the juice that their success at being into the juice is more important to them than whether you think they're neat or not or whatever you may think about them. That's because they usually feel like they're winning, and if they see a thing go down like that episode with the guys from the woodshop and the lady from canning and nobody says anything about it, they assume that all the people there are fools and the reason none of the people said anything about it is because they didn't see it, that they were the only one who saw that and all the rest of those people are fools. That's one of those kind of head trips you can get into, which follows from being into the juice.

You can be into the juice when it's your emergency. You can be the one who got injured and had something happen, and you can be into the juice, too, right on top of it. Sometimes hospital attendants and people like that just shoot people up with big jolts of something for nothing other than being into the juice: Back out, get out from the juice. Okay, *Zap!*

This is a weird metaphor, but suppose the energy comes down through us like little basketballs. Now suppose there's just a rain of energy coming this way in little basketballs. Every time a basketball came, suppose all the people in the front row hit it real hard like a volleyball, and kicked it clear back over the heads of the people in back so it went over all their heads and they didn't get any of it, and then it would be downstream and too late for them to get those balls anymore. Wouldn't that be a funny thing? Suppose somebody came up and took a fence wire, and built a great big funnel so that all the balls funnelled down and just hit them. Suppose somebody came over and stood in front of you and just stood there, and every time one was about to come to you they went *Pow! Pow!* and batted them away.

Or suppose you had a little five-gallon bucket of water you carried around with you all the time, and it was your water, and if it was full you had a lot of water, and if it was empty you didn't have any. Suppose there were some folks who, every time you bumped into them, they'd give you a big hassle and take a quart of your water and split down the road with it.

Suppose there were some folks who didn't have any water and

were getting kind of thirsty and dehydrated and dried out and red-faced and having a hard time and not making it very good because of having no water, and some other folks had gotten together and poured theirs into a big swimming pool and were all swimming. Suppose somebody kicked holes in the side of the swimming pool and let it all run out. Suppose thirsty people who were so thirsty that they didn't have good sense climbed the fence and hurled themselves in the pool. What about that?

Well, don't worry, I ain't gonna leave you hanging there. That was such a heavy lot of supposing. Nobody digs it when anybody was left out. If you find somebody who climbs a fence and hurls himself in the pool and can't swim, you have to rescue him, man. You have to pump him out. You have to help him out.

I've been really familiar with the concept of being into the juice for some dozen years now. It's one of the real good tools in my tool chest. It's all polished from a lot of use, and I've seen a lot of stuff go down. I've been watching a long time. And you see folks do things from being into the juice that would seem unimaginable, stuff that seems so weird or so bizarre or so harsh or so evil or so wrong that you wonder why they do it.

That is why people in this culture have the fascination with violence. One reason is the culture's tremendous bad conscience for having dealt out so much violence to the rest of the world. Nobody feels deep in their heart that we have been what you would call the good guys in the last twenty years. Nobody can make themselves believe that anymore—we have been into the juice of the whole planet.

But we've seen people do things that we couldn't imagine why they'd do it. But you can understand it perfectly if you understand energy and how powerful it is and how attractive it is, how beautiful and how desirable it is, and how necessary it is, like oxygen and water, to everyone, to live properly, healthy and sane. You can see that everyone has to have it or they're not going to be healthy and they're not going to prosper. It's not just a desire or a lust or a sin to love life force and love energy, and to be into the juice in some degree. We live on energy; there ain't nothing good for you that ain't got any energy in it. We live on it. So we spot it, we see it. Anything that we see in our life that means energy to us, shines out to us. When you see beautiful people full of energy, glistening, full of muscles, pretty things on people, that's their energy and their life force, and that's what makes them pretty. That's why beauty is more than skin deep: it's not how long is your nose, it's how much life force have you got; and _any_ of us with enough life force on is beautiful.

Knowing that, we have an obligation to make everyone be pretty. Everybody ought to get to be pretty, because all it takes is juice.

So you have to say, not only that you will not be intimidated, but if someone tries to intimidate you, you will step out in public and be a champion for the people, all the people that that person may be intimidating when you step out in public and bring it out. You can say,

"Hey! This person be's scarey to me, and I want to feel better about that. I don't want to have to be around somebody who feels like they are going to be heavy with me when nobody is looking." Lay it out. When you say it out in the open like that, it helps.

That's how I talked on Haight Street. People were wild on the street to get attention. They would do anything—_anything!_, your wildest and most macabre and weirdest imagination—obviously a pathological condition.

There is loving spirit and then there is sheer, utter disaster. If it weren't for all the folks all over the world who lived through those years, learned something, and ain't going to quit, it would have been a disaster. If we quit, it will have been a disaster, because it cost a bunch. We were taking baths in life force. But now it ain't like you can go on your trip and freak out and hurt yourself without mattering to someone else. We are all interdependent, and we are all taking care of each other. And we have to use our good judgment and our good love and our good courage to do it.

What you're supposed to do is just to love folks un-self-consciously and wholeheartedly and do not define yourself to them, but let them experience you, and don't tell them what to think about you or tell them how to treat you or anything like that. Just put it on them and let them have some. Almost everybody is really grateful for that kind.

Walking with the Landlords

I was wondering if braiding my hair with strips of American flag was too revolutionary, but on the other hand, I felt that I should probably let you know what I looked like in front of the White House and the F.B.I. building while I was there with the Longest Walk. And I hope that was all right.

If you really listened closely to what those people were saying, there was a real composite voice that was coming out of all those different voices from all those different places: from the Muskogee, from Oklahoma; the Lumni from Washington State; the Iroquois up in New York; and the Sioux in Dakota; there was a composite voice that came out of that. It was the voice of a culture, saying,

"There's almost so few of us now that we almost can't keep this culture going. Please don't make there be any fewer of us now. Help us out."

They had a poster that said,

If the last member of a species should die, a whole world has to pass and come again before another such a one can be born.

We felt we were very privileged to be around those people and to get to serve them. I thought James Mejia, one of PLENTY's paramedics from the Bronx, was especially blessed. He got to minister to an old lady who lost a son in the Pine Ridge Wars with the F.B.I. She had gotten faint on the caravan, and James took care of her. And she knew him later on, because she kind of imprinted on him when she came back in. She said,

"I know you, you're the guy that was there."

We got to help out in a lot of ways like that, and I felt like the thing that we were doing there was very simple in a very straight way. The thing I was doing was the thing that Mr. Carter should have been doing: We were going among them, and we were begging for forgiveness.

Some people knew it and some people didn't. A Bishop from the Methodist Church knew it well, and stood up and apologized to the Sioux nation for what the Methodists had done to their culture—assuming that because they were sort of Stone Age and funny through a European eye, that there was no value in their trip, because it seemed unusual or strange or savage.

That's really the strong question going through them right now, because they haven't really got much land left, not nearly enough—but they have some shreds of their culture left, and they try to honor the elders. They're trying to get the young people to honor their elders, trying to get them to pay some attention to these old people who still know the language. They give a lot of juice to anyone who still knows the language. They're very serious about preserving that culture.

When I was at a pow-wow in Minneapolis, I saw a Bird Dancer, kind of a tall, thin dude that was dressed like a bird and knew how to move in bird ways and stuff. I went up to him on the Longest Walk and told him he'd gotten me very stoned with his bird dancing and I could feel the tradition behind it and all that. He told me he was forty-six years old and he had only started dancing two years ago. He said he had decided, as a conscious, grown-up decision, to go take up this art, to take up this craft, this skill, this discipline. When I saw him dancing in Minneapolis, as he moved around the circle of the drum, you could cast your attention into him, your consciousness, and feel the consciousness he was in as he danced—and it would get you high and make you rush and keep you accelerating as long as you paid attention to him. He just had this clean consciousness on him while he went around being that bird.

A lady on the Walk had a miscarriage, a pretty early one, and Leslie Luna—one of our midwives—took her in to the hospital. The Indian lady, after Indian customs, wanted that baby to take home and bury after their ways, and the hospital treated it like it was an appendix or something, and wasn't going to give it up. And Leslie had to report to the Indians that she couldn't get it.

They said, "You'd *better* get it."

They sent her back with three carloads of braves, and they explained that these people had been walking three thousand miles about their religious beliefs, and now was not a good time to hit on them about it.

They wanted to do their ways, and the thing they were trying to explain, again and again, is this: Even the most well-intentioned help, if it destroys their culture, is not help at all. Take an Indian foster kid and turn him into a white kid, and you didn't help him. You may have saved his life, but you made him into a white man. You didn't help him at all. And that went in various levels.

I could make a heart connection with the most radical there, because they are just too native a people not to make the heart connection, regardless of what place they might be in, and no matter what they sound like. One fellow, after we had gotten to D.C. and were in front of the White House, said,

"Well, now that we have done the Longest Walk, I have another idea I would like our white support groups to get behind us with. It is called the Longest Swim."

Which is rather a cold shot. I kept telling them I didn't know where to swim—a leg here and an arm there.

Grandfather David is 104 now. He met up with Fuji Guruji, who was the 93 year-old teacher of the Nam Yo Rengye Ko sect in Japan. Some of his folks went the whole Walk with the Sioux from the very beginning, from Oakland, Alcatraz, and he showed up for the last part, being pushed along in his wheel chair with a Longest Walk bumper sticker stuck to the side of it. He came carrying twenty million signatures from Japanese people against the nukes, from the only country who ever had it used against them. Fuji Guruji wanted to strike a blow about the nukes in the United States, and read a long statement, which was a very clean statement about the nature of the United States' action with the nukes. It was about the myth of sovereignty of governments over the people.

He was representing something like a quarter or a fifth of the population of Japan, with that many signatures. The Sioux, who sit on a reservation with uranium said,

"Okay, you anti-nuclear people. If you want to stop the nukes, you back us up and we will sit on it, and won't let it out of the reservation; we won't sell it. You back us up, we will back you up." It was very strong, in that way.

Dick Gregory addressed them, and it was outrageous. It was

intensely religious throughout. One morning the Navajo, who are properly called the Dine (dee-NAY),had a peyote meeting. Later on that morning, the Indian delegation went in to see Vice-President Mondale, and the Navajo women felt that they wanted to be represented, because they had some strong statements to make about strip-mining and relocation in Navajo territory. So they agreed to give the Navajo ladies first whack at him. So these old Navajo grannies came in with a court brief about two inches thick, slammed it down on the desk so hard it made Mondale jump, and proceeded to chew tail in Navajo for ten or fifteen minutes.

Chief Oren Lyons was telling us what was going on at the meeting, and he said that Mondale was very interested in what the translation of this might be.

It is the way the Indians have of dealing with this, essentially male, government. And it has such a beautiful sense of humor in it, too.

Then we were at the FBI building. The FBI was very funny: we were setting up the p.a., and Philip, our sound man, was over here with a cord in his hand at the bars, waving the cord through the bars at all these people in polyester slacks and sunglasses, saying,

"Could you plug this in right over there? Right over there. . . . See? There it is, right over there . . ." and nobody would look at him or answer him or act like he was there or anything. We were trying to get the electricity out of the feds, with all the most notorious Indian badmouths on the continent standing there at the microphone just champing at the bit. Philip remembered we had an inverter on the camper, and we hooked him up to the back of the camper. It powered the most amazing stuff, all day long.

I didn't mind most of it. Most of it seemed perfectly appropriate. I thought it was okay that the Indians could go in and call out the F.B.I. agents by name that they accused of being *agents provocateurs* on the reservation, which is some of what went down. Louise went around with the long-nosed camera, taking pictures of F.B.I. agents until *they* started taking pictures of *her*.

But it was wrong that the President didn't come out and talk to them. It really shows exactly what they are talking about. He says that he has this agreement with this sect or with that sect, where we had an assembly ranging from the most spiritual leaders like the Six Nations—heavy spiritual leaders, real statesmen, real diplomats—to the political leaders of the Sioux. That group was the traditional people, the political people and the elders, all at once. They represented the Indians, and the President should have been out there.

In particular, they were in Washington to publicize eleven bills that were before Congress. These bills range from termination of all Indian programs, which is one of them, to various and sundry ways of taking their fishing rights, getting their uranium and coal, moving them around—and the Indians are saying they want self-determination and that the white Bureau of Indian Affairs people get to rent Indian land for a dollar an acre to white ranchers to do cattle on, without the consent of the whole tribe. That sort of thing. This series of bills were pretty abusive upon them, and they wanted to make that known. Senator Cranston, who used to be Controller and then got to be Senator in California, Ron Dellums, a Congressman from California, and Teddy Kennedy were the only ones who came out to talk to them. And Cranston said that none of those bills was going to pass, and no senator was taking them seriously.

The Indians were uptight about it, because in the 1950's there was a program called _termination_. All the Indian programs were to be terminated and the Indians were to be assimilated. And the whole point that the Indians are telling everybody about is that they _don't want to be assimilated_. They don't want to be square Americans. They are a nice thing. They like being Indians. And they would like, at this late date, that we back off and give them enough room to be Indians. And the things they _don't_ want us to do is come and build multi-million-dollar culture centers on top of five hundred year-old villages. We should back off and let them Indian a little bit. That is the essence of their position.

The real business I didn't get to see, like when the chiefs spoke with Mondale and senators and various people. There were a lot of talks. But since I couldn't be with them while they were talking with senators, I supported them by going over to the F.B.I. building and being ostentatious. I am really praying for them.

But they know what the battle lines are: Over the next decades, Congress will try to legislate them out of their raw materials, rather than pay for them. And there are two differences of opinion. The government says that it is all Federal Government land which the Great White Father had allotted to the Indians for their use—and that the Great White Father can take it back when he wants it.

And the Indians say, "No, no. Those reservations are the little pieces of land we never gave to you. It was ours back to the Pleistocene and the saber-toothed tiger. We have always been on this land. We have been on this land so long, we are adapted to it."

They point out that there is a sort of distinction about people who have been on the land so long that they are adapted to it. We all have been banging around the world for millions of years, but when you have the right kind of lips and eyes for that sun for that latitude, for roots and berries,—if there is anybody who has any naturals left, who knows where the territory is that they came from at all, they ought to get to live that kind of life.

It would probably help for a bunch of people whose addresses aren't the reservation to write the legislators about preserving what remains of the Indian culture. Ted Kennedy came over to defend his bill—one of the eleven on the list—and he said it wasn't a bad bill, and they had him wrong. It was kind of a scene, out on the lawn by the Washington Monument. The PLENTY ambulance from New York was there, and they were using the p.a. on the ambulance to talk to the meeting with. So Ted Kennedy came up and got the p.a., and talked to the meeting a little bit, and got off pretty clean. He explained two provisions in his bill which have to do with things like if a teenager gets caught in town, he gets turned over to the tribal council and not to the state police. He thought they should appreciate that. I don't know if he misrepresented anything or not, but he managed to say two or three things like that and get a round of applause, and split on the round of applause.

But Russell from the Sioux didn't dig it, and called him back and engaged him in a hassle. They were trading the microphone back and forth, and it was a shouting match—this amazing scene going on.

On some of that stuff, you have to be a specialist to tell exactly where it is at. I think that Ted Kennedy was afraid he was losing ground with those folks and he really came out to make a statement that he was going to try to do better. I think that Jerry Brown not extraditing Dennis Banks is about as strong a statement that any Establishment person has made yet.

They talked about Rosebud Reservation and Pine Ridge Reservation quite a bit in front of the F.B.I. building. It was one of the main topics of conversation. They talked about these shoot-out trips they had been in. I felt sorry for Russell—he had a lot of pain on his face, and he was going to jail in the next day or so. He talked some bitter stuff, as one might who was going to jail that next day or so. And Russell represents a certain kind of grievance that they do have. The F.B.I, the cops, the marshals, have been out to get the Sioux. There has been a real bad feeling in that thing, and they shouldn't have to feel that way.

One of the few white people that they trust is a lawyer named Ken Tilson. The reason they trust him is because he did stuff like sneak through the F.B.I. and B.I.A. Police lines at Pine Ridge to see them. He jumped the lines to get in. They call him their brother. The thing that he liked about the day's action was that they had come here and surrounded the F.B.I. building, to make up for how many times they have been surrounded by the F.B.I.

They are more and more serious about being the guardians, some of the last of the natural people. I think that is one of the strongest things we can learn from them, is just respect for that stuff. They learned a lot about the country, too. There were guys who hadn't been anywhere before, and they walked all the way across the country—and they talked about what they had seen across the country. The first day out across the Coast Range, it got down to ten below and they had to run for fifty miles to stay warm. Many of them had real bad feet because their feet went out back in Kansas, but they were determined to finish the Walk. They were really serious about what they were doing.

The Farm is a White Stick village. It's important to understand that. When I was staying at the Beltway Park with the Indians outside D.C., every day when I went in the gate and saw that red war bonnet with all the red tips on the feathers and the red thingies hanging down the side, I said,

"This is a red-stick camp, Jack." There is an old Indian tradition of the red stick and the white stick camp. A white stick camp is a peaceful village, and if the people decide they want to go to war, they put up a pole and all the folks that want to go to war go hit the pole and move to a Red Stick village. Baton Rouge means red pole, and Baton Rouge was a red stick village, which is a village that went to war. There were other villages that did not go to war; they studied in the arts and tradition and history and religion and didn't go to war—and those were White Stick villages. We're a White Stick village: about as military as we get is medicine and law.

But the Indians don't really think of it the way we think of war. We think of carriers and atomic bombs, jet planes and B-56's and all that old stuff—that's all gross and horrifying and disgusting to them; they really don't understand that level, and what they say is war is like when you have heavy differences that you may have to settle in some forcible fashion, and that war and politics and law are all kind of similar. And that's how come the Indian security wore red threads in their braids. Red was the color of war, and they were security, so they were like some kind of heat, and the red in their braids was like your woven duty belts and your white helmet and white glove and spats and all that.

They had a lot of good support and a lot of friendly people. I was always trying to tell them they had good support and let them know it, because they didn't always get to find it out. But their security was a little over-enthusiastic at first, to where their security was almost as bad as the cops. The security was mainly any guy who had the nerve to braid a red thread in his hair or wear a red armband and say that he was security. By the time they got to D.C., they had the reporters backed off so far they were hardly getting any press at all, because they had scared the press away so bad. A discussion went on about that, and some of the Six Nations elders spoke to the whole camp about it. Oren Lyons spoke about it. Then they let the press up to get some pictures of some of the people and the elders, and they got a lot better relations with the press after that. But there was so much heart in the walkers and so little of it getting out that they got frustrated. They felt no one was paying enough attention to what they were trying to state.

They want a lot, and a lot of it they should get, because it is just so insane. If they can't live in this world, it is going to be unfit to live in. That is really the message they bring—if it isn't going to be fit for them, it isn't going to be fit for anyone. We all have to regenerate and touch the real thing now and then.

Back from Australia

I never thought I'd be standing in the middle of New Zealand talking to a couple of hippies wearing loincloths, and discussing the advantages of the United States Constitution. It's different to live under a monarchy than it is to live under a constitution. You can tell the difference. You can feel it. It's really noticeable.

One of the things that's almost scary is to see to what extent the scene that's happening in the U.S. leads the world. In Australia, especially, the people there have been toured by everybody that tours the U.S., and they just ritually believe all of it. They believe a lot of funny stuff, trying to do it like the U.S. It's funny, because they don't realize that they *have been* leaders, and *could continue to be*. Australia got out of the war in Viet Nam some time before we did. They were a little ahead of us. And it was a privilege of ours to be associated with the man who helped make it so that they got out of the Viet Nam war earlier, Dr. Jim Cairns. He was Deputy Prime Minister at the time of the demonstrations against the war in Viet Nam, and there were about twenty thousand people going to the demonstrations. He went to them, and when he went they swelled to about a hundred thousand, and it made a big difference. It helped swing the weight that way.

They feel cut off from the rest of the world, in some sense, and they've accepted a lot of things by way of rip-offs and brand-names. It's funny, because all the various companies have glommed each other's brand names down there. They're far enough away that nobody pays attention to brand names very much, so they rip each other off terrible. They figure anything from the United States is pretty much up for grabs. That makes me really understand why we have to be so careful to send out a very clear signal. It's really important that we send out something really clear, because the people in Australia were really very happy to hear from us. There's only fourteen million of them down there in that pretty big continent, but the Continental Divide is only a hundred and fifty miles in from the coast, and the rest of the continent is mostly desert.

And of all the things to happen, strange as it may be—I don't know who writes the script for these things—they found that thirty per cent of the world's high-grade uranium supply is under the Aborigines' reservation.

Again.

So they're having this tremendous controversy down there, and at various times people like the truckdriver's union doesn't want to move any uranium, and they don't have any reactors there, so if they moved it at all, it would just be in the position of selling something they didn't use themselves. So there's a tremendous controversy in the country going on about that.

The youth movement is split up into three different groups, which is one of the reasons they don't have a stronger thing than they have. They're split up into the health-fooder hippies, the surfers who have the technology—the surfer wagons and the mystique—and the punks. The punks are the revolution, but they're not a viable lifestyle. The surfers are almost a viable lifestyle except they're living on the dole—but all of them have economy-size panel truck surfer wagons; they've got the highest young people's technology level. The hippie health-fooder group has no technology whatsoever. And as far as their grasp of the scientific method goes, I found that it was not the aborigines who went,

"One, two, three, . . . many," but the Australian hippies. The Aborigines had much more depth than that.

It's very interesting to go to other countries where the seed has been scattered, and see that sometimes different seed is strong, as far as having a material plane manifestation together. Some of the strongest things showing on New Zealand were the Hare Krishnas and the Hare Krishna splinter group. They'd split into two groups on that island, and they both had a big tent, and one of them had a big bus and like that. All around the world in different places, the manifestation is at different levels, at different points in time. And this is known to the people who have planetary viewpoints. But it is not known to the general citizenry of all of these individual countries.

In New Zealand, they have a hippie scene that's like stepping into a time machine and finding yourself in Marin County in the 'Sixties. It's down by the ocean and it's nice, and the weather's nice. There's a bunch of hippies. They pull fifteen or twenty thousand to a festival out of a country that only has three million people. That's a pretty big percentage of the country that turned out for it.

In New Zealand, they have a pretty strong bus and van scene. In Australia, the dole is pretty easy to get and it seems like a lot of the people are pretty sapped in their ability to do anything—they tend to be pretty superstitious about health and self-care and stuff like that, because they're not really doing it. In New Zealand, it seems to be a lot harder to get on the dole, and they seem to have a stronger bus and van scene, which is evidence of people trying to take care of themselves.

The festival in Australia was sort of middle-class folks trying to do a love-in on about five square miles of what looked like the Mojave Desert. It was some of the roughest territory I ever saw people actually try to do something on. But the one in New Zealand was thrown by a bunch of hippies who wanted to have a good party, and they were trying to make it as nice as they could make it. They weren't trying to conceptually rough it or anything like that. The folks who try to conceptually rough it usually go a little bit too far towards roughing it.

They have these flies in Australia. They're the most amazing flies. They're not as big as American flies, and they don't buzz as loud, and they're not the sort that buzz you like a helicopter, like American flies do; but these flies land on your face and they don't go away when you brush at them or when you blow at them. If you touch them, they just walk over a little ways. They just land and go up onto your nose.

I saw a picture in a magazine that does an Around-the-World section. And it had a picture of an Aborigine with a fly sitting on the corner of one of his eyes and it said,

"Aborigine ignoring fly with characteristic indifference."

After having been down in Australia for a while, I have a picture in my camera which I hope will come out. I tried to get a picture of the ex-Deputy Prime Minister ignoring fly on third eye with characteristic indifference.

They say that you can tell when you get the television station from the state capital, because the guy that does the news will be fanning flies away from his face while he's talking.

It was a scene at that festival in Australia. It was such a relief to go over to New Zealand and find a thing with a lot of love put into things like making a nice big-produced stage, a good set of lights, and they had a bunch of bands that can play rock and roll.

We need to go learn some tribal ways from some of these folks that still have them.

There's this little island of two million people—well, two little islands. One of the islands is very very English and doesn't have very many Maori people, and it has Alps with snowcaps on them. It's like a little island Switzerland stuck down in the South Seas. And the other island has a bunch of Maori people on it, who are a Polynesian people who look a lot like American Indians.

One of the main things I noticed about New Zealand was that most of it is logged. You can go look at the most remote places in the world, and man has been there and left a big old mark. They have trees in New Zealand that grow fifteen hundred and two thousand years old—Kowrie trees. And the Kowrie tree is your basic jungle giant. They grow seventy feet to the first branch, and are thirty feet in girth. It's a huge, gigantic old thing. They logged them back in 1912 and 1918 and like that. On up into the 'Sixties, they logged these things. It was like logging redwoods. There's still a few of the old loggers around, and they tell stories of the mighty labors they did. But in your heart you kept thinking you wished they'd just left them alone, and left those old jungle giants grow. We got to drive through a piece of woods that hadn't been cut down and look at a few of them that were still standing, and feel that same presence. We saw this tree that was called the God of the Forest. And it was. You could tell.

We went through Nimbin in Australia. Nimbin is the place where they had the festival four or five years ago that was like their Woodstock. And two or three thousand people or more stayed in that area. The little local town of Nimbin had all the storefronts done up with psychedelic paint jobs and stuff, and they had quite a web of culture there. The only trouble is that they're all on the dole, or most of them anyway, and the neighbors are uptight about it. That was the subject of the conversation that I had with them a great deal of the time.

They kept saying, "What do you think we could do to get our community together so it will be strong?"

And I said, "Get off the dole."

And they said, "Besides that."

And folks would give me the most amazing rationalizations about it. They would say,

"Well, it doesn't really come from those guys who are doing the working, it just looks like it does—it's actually all from the government."

And I kept saying, "There's some dude that goes to work at a car plant who makes a deal to sell his labor at x amount of dollars an hour, and when his check comes to him he doesn't get it all. There's a little piece of it missing, and you get it."

It was hard to say anything different than that. Since we left, I heard that a lot of people were really taken by that idea, and some changes were going down.

There's been a lot of stuff through Australia. New Zealand hasn't had as much stuff through there. It makes for an interesting difference in the scene. Australia is a little burnt. They've had a lot of stuff happen to them. The reason their punk rockers are so strong is that people are so burnt with gurus and stuff like that. The punk rockers talk about how much they're down on hippies. But I was talking one night to a bunch of people, and there was a punk-rocker in the audience who had short hair that was turquoise and green and orange and red, and maybe a little silver.

I said, "Gee, I didn't know about you guys' trouble with your government. We didn't even know you had a government."

And this guy says, "We 'aven't."

I saw more and more that one of the truest and heaviest things we can do is back up the native people of the world. That's one of the strongest all-around-the-world unifying principles that young people like us can get together and have a strong, good vibe behind. Because the story is the same everywhere you go. It's not just that the people are actually in danger; the danger is in losing those cultures. Even before it gets to a level where the people are in danger, there is the level of where the cultures are gone.

While we were in New Zealand, they buried a lady with full tribal honors. The New Zealanders are really a lot like the American Indians. Birds were their main thing, so they're into feathers and stuff, even. So they had these feathered cloaks, and they walked up this real steep hill, with several people having to haul the casket up the hill with ropes, and no white people allowed on the property. And who they were burying was the last lady alive who remembered their last king. She's a link. She's the last link with something in their history. It was heavy for all the people in the island to bury that old lady. She was the last lady old enough to remember the Maoris' own last king, when they were last their own people. And the people really wanted to make that a Holy and sacred time.

There are 180,000 Australian Aborigines left. 180,000.

I found that folks who were burnt by spiritual things and felt that way, sometimes questioned me very closely about what was my religion. When it comes down to my own personal religion, my religion is this one that's happening right now. It still ain't got no name yet. When I'd say that, I got cheers and stomps and whistles from crowds that were hostile to religion. They would all be willing and ready to admit that there was a religiousness in the hearts of the people, that didn't have a name on it yet and it was just all around in all our hearts, and that's the only place it lived was in the hearts of the people. And if it didn't live there, it didn't live.

In Australia, when you call somebody heavy, you call them "Uncle." You don't call an aboriginal priest "Father," you call him "Uncle." I got to meet an Aborigine initiated man, Uncle Ted. He's like a Holy man. He showed us his Family Tree. It was as if I walked out to the third oak tree from the left and said,

"This is my Family Tree."

He got me over there and said, "See that tree?" and there was this eucalyptus tree, and he said, "That's our Family Tree." And the far-out thing about it was that there was nothing whatsoever to distinguish that eucalyptus tree from any other eucalyptus tree in the forest, except that it was his Family Tree. It was far out, because it didn't mean that that tree was any less Holy on account of being like all the other trees. It meant that all of the other trees were Holy, too.

Uncle Ted and his Family Tree

He showed us this big old craggy rock and said, "Now the name of that rock over there," and he told me this name. Aboriginal names are kind of hard to remember, just because I'm not used to them. So he told me this long name about what the name of this place was, which I couldn't remember, and then he saw that I couldn't remember. He wanted to help me out, so he told me what that name meant. And what that name meant was so simple and un-conceptual that I may not remember the word, but I'll always remember the definition. He said,

"You see that rock over there with all those trees growing on it? Well, the name of that place means 'good place for stuff to hide in.' "

Most of the stuff he was pointing out to me meant that kind of thing. He's really a good dude.

Down there they don't say rap, they say rave. "I want to rave to you, mate." Uncle Ted had a great rave, and his thing was that he'd never been to the first grade. He'd gone to work in a foundry as a laborer when he was young, and he worked at this foundry for many years. In the course of working at the foundry, he got to shovel sand for the molds and casts. Then, pretty soon they started letting him make some of the molds, letting him pour some of the stuff into the molds. And in the course of years working there, he worked himself up to being a die maker, and got to a pretty high level of the craft. And he knows he never went to the white man's school, he never went to the first grade. He just did it with his own Aborigine brain. He moved to a high level of a high craft, and he knows it just as good. And he knows that an Aborigine head is just as good as an Englishman's head, and he knows it good in his heart. He's got a good rave on account of that, because he's not afraid to say what he believes, and he's strong in his own thing. I gave him pictures of the Indians presenting themselves at Geneva, and he turned on to them so strong and talked about how much he loved those people. We just got to be better and better friends by the second. Even as we were getting ready to go, we were still getting to be better friends. He says,

"Wait a minute. I've got to get you something," and he runs back to the house and comes out with his headband. He said he never goes to a Holy place without wearing his headband. He brings me his headband and gives me a thumbs-up hippy handshake. Tribal

friends with some tribal people.

We had some funny initiations. Another sort happened to Ina May, when we met these guys at the festival at Nambassa in New Zealand. At the festival in Australia, they hadn't had sufficient medical because they had been so superstitious about it. The only medical they had was extreme hippie color therapy and stuff like that, and it's hard to do color therapy for having stepped on a broken bottle.

But over at the festival in New Zealand where the hippies were trying to take care of themselves, they engaged the St. John's Ambulance Service, which is a free thirteen-hundred-year-old order of Emergency Medical Technicians. They are the medical side of the Knights of Malta. The Knights of Malta were the Knights of Amalfi, and the Amalfi cross was carried to the Crusades. And those guys were medics in the Crusades. They came back and then they went to the island of Malta, which is why that's known as the Maltese Cross. These guys were the ambulance, and they were great. They had on uniforms. They wore shorts—all the uniforms in the South Pacific were shorts, except in Fiji and Tahiti, where they wear skirts, which is kind of neat, to see a guy set up with a regular airline uniform and a skirt. But this guy from the St. John's Ambulance Service gave Ina May one of his pins off his uniform and said,

"This is actually called a mufti pin, it's the one you wear when you're in the Order, but not wearing the uniform," and he pinned it on her and made it like she was one of them.

You already know who are your brothers, because that's the folks that you run into who are out there doing the thing.

I realized that we, too, have an order of free Emergency Medical Technicians. Maybe we'll be a thousand-year-old order some day.

In New Zealand, they were real nice guys and really spiritual, and really serious. Their festival came out really well, and it was like a good scene with no hassle, man. There was one small motorcycle outbreak of the Maori Filthy Few. Their Hell's Angels are the Filthy Few. The Filthy Few are pretty heavy. I was walking through the festival when I saw the Filthy Few. They had to tell me what their name was because their jackets were so dirty I couldn't read the back. There was a _hangi_, or cookout pit, near my feet, and I looked down as I passed. As I did, they said,

"Don't step in, or we might just cook you."

They're like Cochese or Geronimo or somebody back there at the fringes of Arizona fighting it out with the pony soldiers. They're just folks on the edge of that island. I don't think they want to go back to living completely the way they were before the white man came, although it wasn't that bad a life.

New Zealand is an amazing place. There weren't any mammals on that place before the year one thousand. No mammals, just birds. The only mammals were bats. The only critters on the island were the ones that flew there. The white man brought in dogs, rats, pigs, goats, all kinds of deer, and stotes, which is a kind of weasel. Now they have goats in the woods, and there were people in the community there whose main disagreement with my scene was that they wanted to shoot goats and pigs, because they were overrun with them. It was the old life-and-death argument, but it was one of those things where we were arguing about whether to shoot the goat and pigs, and not only were they saying they were going to shoot them, but they were going to eat them. It made me feel strange because right in the middle of that, this baby choked on a green bean, and it was one of those big scenes where we got the green bean out of the baby. It was one of those fast, sudden things that come on to you, and I thought,

"I wish I'd gone into this scene differently."

It was okay, and it came out okay, but I wished I hadn't had to be arguing about life and death for the past hour. And they didn't really understand or make that connection, or notice that *it's funny to be out of position when something happens.*

We think that England is just like us because they speak English; but that's an illusion and a kind of ethnocentricity to think that. Seeing Australia is a really different thing, because it lets you see a country that's almost like a Third World country in some ways, except it speaks English. I keep talking about how American law comes from English common law, and it does, but Australia and New Zealand have not had their independence yet, and you can tell by the way people are; you can tell that it ain't as free.

In other ways, you can tell just by the way people are, that ultimately, when things go up for grabs, the process of government just breaks down. Like when Watergate happened, it fell into the hands of such complete gangsters and crooks and unscrupulous people that they couldn't tolerate this government at all; and the government just went up for grabs. When it went up for grabs in America, what it fell into is the Constitution, which tells you what to do next when your government goes up for grabs.

Down in Australia, four years ago, they had an election and elected a socialist government. And these guys were really going to do the socialist thing, but they did it a little too fast and they scared some people somewhat by coming on so strong. They did things like hiring women for advisory positions, and trying to do something for the Aborigines. There was no government agency that had anything to do with the Aborigines until this socialist government went in. In all the history of Australia, there has been no government agency about Aborigines, and the people have been allowed to do to them pretty much what they wanted to, without government interference. Up until two years ago or so.

Uncle Ted Thomas, the Aboriginal elder, told me that the people of South Africa are the most oppressed people that he knows about, but he said,

"We're next, right after them. The world attention should be focused on them because they need it; and us next, right after them."

So this government is at a place where Australia, New Zealand, and Canada were all parts of England. They used to be just colonies of England, and then they said they were going to be a different kind of a status—it was going to be a commonwealth and they weren't going to be like colonies any more. They were going to have a certain level of independence: They were going to be commonwealths.

That meant that things changed, because it used to be that there was a Governor-General, and that the Governor-General was the Queen's direct representative. The Queen appointed the Governor-General and he could do anything he wanted to with the country. There was also a government which ran the country, and the Prime Minister was the head of the government which ran the country. When they changed them into being a commonwealth, it looked as if the office of Governor-General had become an honorary office of sorts. They gave it to 80-year-old people with a Sir in front of their name, in the proper costume who would ride at the head of a parade for a couple of blocks during ceremonies and stuff.

They thought that's all there was to it, and instead of being appointed by the Queen any more, because they were a commonwealth, the Governor-General was going to be appointed by the Prime Minister, since they were a country now.

So they had this left-wing Prime Minister, and he appointed a right-wing Governor-General.

Then the Governor-General up and fired the Prime Minister and fired the Labor government. It blew everybody's minds.

They hadn't realized that when it goes up for grabs, it doesn't fall back on the Constitution. It falls back on the Queen. And the Queen's representative took precedence over the elected government and was able to fire the Prime Minister and the Labor government. The people's elected government could just up and be fired.

We were right in the middle of that, because Jim Cairns, the guy who had us over to Australia, was the ex-Deputy Prime Minister of that government, who had gotten fired himself a couple of months before the government. He went out a little early. People in the Movement are very bitter, because they actually elected what they wanted once and got it fired out from under them. They're bitter, and don't know what to do about it. They consider it to be a *coup* that just happened to them. It makes it so that the Revolution is angry and bitter and not very effective—more in the nature of something that's being done to the Conservatives to show them, rather than something that's being done for themselves to raise the condition. That's a hard way for it to be, but that's what it feels like in Australia.

And the Queen, by her silence, allowed it to go down. That was her representative, and she never said anything about it. She acted like she was just above it or something, and she didn't say anything about it. A little while later, they brought her through on a tour and they did stuff like remodel the faces of the streets that she's going to go down so they'll look good to her.

This is a funny thing. The Queen is not a figurehead. The Queen is the actual repository for that kind of material-plane social position, for real. She is the richest woman in the world, and she doesn't want to let go of none of it. She ain't kidding. It really

made me understand the Beatles a lot stronger when they said,
Her Majesty's a very nice girl,
But she hasn't got a lot to say.

Considering how she lets it go down, she is powerful. She is a powerful figure, and she does not have to let it go down the way she lets it go down, but she lays back and acts like she ain't doing anything, and she is. She's strong. That's what I found out. Royalty lives. I discovered that.

The Australian press is mostly owned by families whose names are all full of Sirs and Orders of the British Empire and Knights of the Bath, except for Murdoch. The press is _managed_, man, and it's outrageous. I squawk about the American press, because our press is a little out of control. But their press is really _controlled_, and doesn't say the heavy stuff. The new Prime Minister even said,

"Let's get cricket back on the front pages, out where it belongs."

They have a little underground press, but it's not much and they have to be fairly cool.

It's funny to be fighting the medical battle we're fighting here in Tennessee, where we're considered to be the extreme idiot hippie left-wing lunatic fringe, and go down into the Australian scene and they treat us like the right wing.

Folks were very flower-childy there. A lot of folks after the one festival we went to, were just folks from the city who were having kind of a vacation. So they were all in kind of conceptual outdoor costumes. This one guy was going to do it like an Aborigine, so he's not wearing anything except a red string around his waist, and from this red string is hanging a bare, sharp butcher's knife. Just this red string and this bare sharp butcher knife hanging there. It was the kind of thing where everyone who walked by had to stop for a second and look and be sure he was all right. It kept being such a hang-up that I finally had to tell him about it. I said,

"Do you realize how careful you have to be to have that bare blade hanging there to be sure you don't gut yourself on it? Doesn't that incapacitate you from being able to do anything besides just watch and be sure you don't cut yourself all the time?"

It was funny to see that sort of thing going on, because I guess the management hadn't expected me to be like I was, or as noisy as I am, and then I kept proceeding on the assumption that if you did it right, you could actually make a community with those people on that dirt. But later on, I came to find out that they hadn't even checked the water rights. The place was complete desert—there was a blade of grass maybe every eighteen inches, and it was dry and dead, and they hadn't checked the water rights. They were at a level of complete material-plane flower-child incompetence, to the point where they just weren't going to do anything that was going to last very long, because they were going to fall apart. That didn't reflect the greater scene in Australia, but that reflected the management of that festival.

It was a good lesson anyway, because the people that came looked at it and saw that it's got to be better than that if we're going to do it, but it was so outrageous that when I gigged the last time in Australia, in Sydney, the last question of the evening I got was a guy who said,

"Do you think that, inasmuch as what it looks like they did was gather all the hippie power in Australia and negate it and make it so it wasn't worth very much, do you think that the jam was thrown by the CIA to break the heart of the hippie movement in Australia?"

I had to say I didn't believe it was that. I thought it was just ignorance.

We did our best, but finally we took off to Nimbin to be with the hippies for New Years. We got there and just came in the middle of a huge New Years party, and they played *Tennessee Mountain Home* and *Rum and Coca-Cola* in our honor . . . and had a rock and roll New Years with the hippies.

There was a lady in Nimbin who had run down to an incredibly bad condition. She was crazy for a start, and when I say she was crazy, I don't mean your old neurotic head trip. I mean when I looked in this lady's eyes, I was instantly transported to the astral plane, *Zap!* She was strong as she could be and she looked at me and looked gently at my forehead and said,

"Oh, I see you're concerned about my condition."

That was right on top of it, except a little nutty. I knew exactly where she was coming from. It turned out she had been allowed to run down. She had rheumatic fever and she got to a place where she got so sick she scared her husband, and he went to one of the other little hamlets—which is what they call a group of houses on one of the other pieces of land—and said,

"My wife's so sick I'm scared. Come see."

So they came, and she was laying out on the floor and so stiff she could hardly move. They took her into the hospital and she had rheumatic fever, and they put her under medication and she had responded somewhat, and was back out of the hospital for a visit the day I saw her.

When she read my mind so cleanly and perfectly as soon as I looked into her eyes, I just relaxed and decided to head-trip with her for a while. She saw I was kind of doing it with her, and she just started saying,

"Well, the trouble with these other people here is that they're not telepathic with me. If these other people were telepathic with me, well, I need a thousand things I don't have time to ask for. They should be buzzing around like a hive of bees, getting me everything I need. These people should all be out here getting it together for me, because I'm the old dying Queen."

She's laying it on me, and I'm going, uh-huh, uh-huh, but she thinks I'm agreeing with her, too, down the line, because I'm also going uh-huh, so she also assumes that she's got me completely head-copped because I keep agreeing. So she starts issuing some very specific orders at this point.

I said, "Whoa, baby. You're pretty tough, but you're not that tough." So we started negotiating from that level for a while, and it was a trip, and the power on her was really zinging, but she was like the Gollum in the Tolkien _Trilogy_, firmly stuck in the Ring of Power and getting crazier by the minute. So we had some pretty good changes, and I told her that those folks who had taken her into the hospital were afraid they had interfered with her free will. I said that the folks who took her to the hospital were known as her friends, and that was how she could tell they were her friends—they were the ones who didn't let her croak, and took her to the hospital, and that she should be really grateful. And I considered those people to be some of the heroes of that community, to go against such a powerful cultural set that the community had against dealing with doctors or anybody, to get that lady into the hospital before she just died on them. They had gotten the flower-child thing out to the extreme where it's dangerous.

I since heard that she recovered.

It was interesting to see the hippie culture in that stage.

The Web of Life

Some of the laws you find in the old books were about things like keeping the people healthy, taking care of the people. In a culture where water was very precious, more for drinking than washing, and where there weren't any antibiotics if you caught anything, you just had to live through it and either you got it or it got you; you survived everything that didn't kill you—there were laws about things that weren't good to eat, for example, because it tended to get you sick in the long run.

In thinking about our tribal ways, it's from that kind of a place that we look at it when we get involved with the nuclear fuel and war cycle in this country. We're coming from a place where religion and public health meet.

To understand it properly, we have to go out to our biggest, widest viewpoint, and really get out there and look in on it, to understand the whole system.

We're here in this Universe. And what we know about this Universe is multifaceted. We know that Canada's up north, Gulf of Mexico's more or less south, California's out there, East Coast's the other way. . . . We know that. And then there's Sol, Type G star, a little old and yellowing, but still got a lot of good stuff. Besides, we probably couldn't even survive around the real white ones—they'd probably fry our genes out so fast we wouldn't even make it. But this one's pretty good. It's pretty dull, doesn't fry us too hard, has a little air to buffer it. It's a nice, safe distance for nuclear energy, 93,000,000 miles.

And all that's sitting in another thing, much bigger than that. We think we're fairly hot because we've been to the moon, but the moon is only a quarter of a million miles away. A quarter of a million miles is hardly anything these days. We took pictures of Venus and our solar system, all on the order of a million miles distant, or five million miles.

And then you go to the nearest star neighbor, 4½ light years away. A light year is how far light can travel in a year, at 186,000 miles per *second*. It's 4½ light years to the nearest star, and that's *close*. Most of these distances, when you get out there, get bigger and bigger and bigger, until we ain't very big or very special. Now, they broke Galileo on the wheel for saying that. They took an honest scientist who said,

"According to my observations, the Earth seems to move."

And they said, "According to our Book, the Earth is the center of the Universe and God's own footstool, and it does *not* move, you heretic." And they put him on the rack and stretched him for saying that it moved.

But it's even worse than that. It's not just that it moves; but it's not even in a very well-populated corner of the Universe. It ain't very hot stuff at all, in an immense, huge-beyond-thought system of systems of systems, of which we only know the very edge. And somewhere, floating around in all this stuff, is this rock that we're on, and this rock is about eight thousand miles thick, and here we are on it. And according to our observations, we have not yet seen anybody from anywhere else that we're sure enough of. They certainly haven't come in and said, "Take me to your leader," yet.

But on this rock there exists a fragile layer. If this Earth was the size of a pool ball like you shoot pool with, all the mountains, from Everest at nearly 30,000 feet, and the five and six mile depths of the ocean, all those surface irregularities would be smoother than the surface of a pool ball. Those irregularities would be unnoticeable to the naked eye; they would be microscopic. And then there is this little fuzz about thirty feet high that sticks up around here—a little fuzz like a mold on the rock or something. The oceans on that pool-ball-size Earth would be thinner than the film if you blew your breath on the ball. And somehow, on this unimportant rock, during natural occurrences, apparently, as far as we know, chemical combinations, electrical combinations, moistures and drynesses, lightnings, formed and re-formed and re-formed, and, as near as we can tell, got lucky and hit something and ticked it over to a new order of stuff. It made it be alive.

Scientists have opinions about when this went down. They say that all of us living critters have 0.9% saline in our blood—that we have 0.9% salt in the water we're made out of. At one time, the oceans were that amount of saltiness, and we apparently evolved from that ocean of 0.9% saline solution—that our blood and the ocean's blood is the same blood, but ours took a little turn. The ocean stayed soup, and we became life. And through changes so long, taking so much time that it staggers the mind and staggers the imagination to try to estimate how long it takes and how many times you are talking about for it to hit just right—we have survived as a little film of protoplasmic slime on the surface of this rock for all of these millions and billions of years. Every one of us who is here is the result of an unbroken string of throwing heads every time, every time. From the Beginning until now, you haven't thrown tails once, or you wouldn't be here. Just once takes you out of the game.

So we have this delicate balance, this interconnected web network of life that the scientists call the biosphere, the little circle, the little thin shell of stuff that lives on the rock. Not too thick in some places, when you think that every blade of grass represents 4,000 miles of rock underneath it that it has to integrate, that it's responsible for life. If you look at every blade of grass that way, you see that in the larger general scheme of things, which is independent of whether anybody cares about the survival of life on this planet, in the larger scheme, every blade of grass and its genetic secrets and its code and its uniqueness is _absolutely necessary_ in the overall picture, and that all of us may have had an ancestor humbler than that blade of grass—and if it had fallen to a lawnmower, maybe none of us could be here. We are that interrelated and that interconnected—and the miracle of Life comes out to be here.

And now we come to the place where we have brought forth a man-made substance. My physics teacher in college had been Madame Curie's lab assistant. Marie Curie was the first scientist to isolate radioactive stuff, and you know what it did? It killed her. She isolated an amount of radioactivity which was named after her, the curie, and at one time all the radioactivity in the world was natural or buried or still in the ores, except for the little bit that she had. And from that time, we have created and mined out of the earth tons and tons and tons and tons and tons and hundreds and thousands of tons of that stuff, and we have refined it and refined it down to its most virulent and poisonous concentrations—and from there we have loosed it back into the world, one way or another.

Now this delicate balance that we call Life exists in a relationship with what we call background radiation. Life and background radiation coexist. If there were no background radiation, there might not be that much evolution. Background radiation is all of the radiation that comes to us from every source other than man-made. The sun, fortunately ninety-three million miles away, is far enough that most of its stuff is a little mellowed, and a lot of its particles never reach this far. And out in space, every star is also emitting particles. Some of the stars are so much hotter than the sun that the sun is almost an old clinker compared to them. They are incredibly hot. Who knows what elements live in those hot stars for only fractions of time. And from there come particles flying through space—cosmic rays. Just particles of stuff flying through space, and nothing to stop it until it gets to you. And you don't even stop it: It just blows right through you, punching a hole so small that you never notice the hole.

Most of the time, that particle doesn't make much difference. Most of the stuff we're made out of is water and empty space anyway, but once in a while, out of all the incredible mathematics of statistics and odds that are possible to calculate about a subject like this, one of those thingies from out there strikes someone in the next egg or the next sperm that is going to take life. Sometimes.

Well, now, those odds seem pretty far out, for one of those little suckers coming from all the way out there in outer space to come get you in the next one up, but everybody here has scores of eggs or millions of sperms, and there are 4½ billion of this kind of creatures. And not only humans have sperms and eggs and chromosomes, but every animal that walks and lives and breathes, and every living tree and grass has protoplasm, chromosomes, made out of the same kind of stuff. And when you look at the odds for some of that stuff coming through space so that part of that giant shower hits some of those cells, it gets more likely.

You can measure cosmic rays with a cloud chamber, which is a device where you pull a vacuum inside a little chamber with some moisture in it, and pull it into a cloud. If a cosmic ray hits that cloud, the particle leaves a little trail through the cloud, and you can see it, like a jet vapor trail. With a simple cloud chamber—it just takes a suction bulb to pop the vacuum on again—you can sit there and you can see a couple of rays hit almost every time you look. They're thick enough that you can sit there, make a little vacuum in a chamber six inches square, and you'll see two or three particles come through it every time you do it. That may help you understand how thick cosmic radiation is. And that's just cosmic radiation.

Then you consider background radiation, of the kind that you measure with a geiger counter—when you have your counter out there and your needle moves over, you know you have something. But as you're listening to that geiger counter, consider that each click you hear is a particle, and it's being hit dozens, hundreds, thousands of times, and that the sensor which is being hit that many times is only an inch or so around— if that square inch is being hit so many times that it can move the needle and make audible sounds, what about every other square inch, which is also full of just as much of it as that little square inch that's going click-click-click.

We live in radiation soup. We are creatures who live in radiation stew. It may be our blesing and it may be our downfall, because we are so delicate and our form, our life, our genetic code, our billions-of-years bank account of our genetic pool, our actual heritage of life, lives in coexistence with that background radiation—and everything that you turn loose into the world adds to that background radiation. Every time you have an atomic bomb like Nagasaki or Hiroshima, every time you have a peacetime test like Frenchman's Flats and Bikini and Alamogordo, New Mexico, and every time you drop an atomic- powered satellite down through the atmosphere and burn up a few hundred pounds of uranium into the atmosphere and every time you explode an atomic submarine like the _Thresher_—which apparently had a meltdown while they were under water, and turned that much radiation loose into the ocean—every time that happens, it adds to the background radiation.

Life organizes, and background radiation is random. There is a balance between life and randomness, and mankind is tampering with the balance, to the point where there is a severe question whether life can survive at all. Not merely whether you'll keep looking like your grandfather, but whether we'll keep on being anything at all. It's not that your kids are liable to have two heads if you get irradiated. 99% of all mutations are lethal,—99% of all possible mutations just kill you—and in that remaining 1% is all the freaky stuff that you hear about and see, that even comes far enough to reach that much fruition. And it has been pointed out that the reproductive efficiency of mankind is not very high, as animals go. Some animals reproduce very accurately with very high percentages. The reproductive efficiency of mankind is only 31%. We can't afford to mess with it real bad.

Another trouble with genes is that some of them are not just injured and that's it; some of them are ones that can reproduce. So you can not only have something that's wrong, but something that's going to *reproduce* wrong, too. It's changed the code.

I get more religious thinking about how this was all a product of fair chance and randomness than I do from somebody going *Zap!* and making it, because I have to stretch my head further to understand it—that this thing goes on long enough for *all* the eventualities to happen, for there to be change in an orderly way. And we don't want to be static. We want to evolve, but just not *too fast*, man. We haven't really finished exploring this kind of monkey and body yet. Let's don't turn into starfish or something quite yet—not for a couple of generations.

The entire genetic pool of the planet is really at stake. Most people know how it works with Siamese cats. The Siamese traits are what they call double-recessive. It means that both cats have to be Siamese or it doesn't look like a Siamese, and won't have the Siamese characteristics. And the hassles with Siamese come because the characteristics are on a double-recessive gene; after breeding Siamese for a long time, they have some of them that are cross-eyed—they look just like Siamese, but they're cross-eyed. Other ones have a little kink in the tail. Those are just genes that are preserved in the heritage of Siamese cats; and you can't get rid of those genes very well, because you have to be double-recessive to even have the ears and tail points and everything come out.

Another instance of mankind messing around, is that there are certain kinds of dogs that we have bred to the point where they can't reproduce without man. Fancy Boxers, great big chest, big-headed dogs, small rear end, just can't give birth. They have to be cesarean. So we've bred a breed of dogs into where they have to be delivered by cesarean all the time. Well, there aren't going to be any of that kind of dogs if there aren't people around to give them cesareans. We've done that to dogs. We've changed their gene pool. We've changed that animal's genetic structure. The Great Dane is another one like that. Great Danes only live about seven years, because their hearts are not in proportion with the size of their bodies. They were bred up to be big dogs, but their hearts are not as heavy-duty as their bodies. It's like a Cadillac body on a Pinto motor, and this is another case where mankind has messed with the genetic structure of some other kind of animal. But mankind, when he messes with atomics, messes with his _own_ gene structure, and you don't know what he'll make.

And if there's any religion in naturalness at all, we ought to let these dice that have been rolling for these millions of years continue to roll and play the game out fair without somebody reaching out and grabbing them and changing the way they're going to go—especially without our permission.

There is no accurate estimation of how many miles that radiation went from the Three Mile Island plant. There's a bunch of differing opinions about it. They say they detected stuff 20 miles downwind. Syracuse, New York, reported it had four times background radiation. State of New York came in and told Syracuse as a city to shut up. People said there was radiation as far as Baltimore. Those were immediate measurements. But of the stuff that came out, some of it had a short half-life and will just die out right away; it will blow for a few miles and then it will be burned up by the time it lands anywhere. But other of that stuff will just kick around indefinitely. It's not going to go away, it's going to keep doing it for thousands of years. It could blow across the Atlantic. That's why, in Europe and in Germany, the demonstrators said,

"We all live in Pennsylvania."

We learned something when Jerry Brown told them to shut

down the nuke that was twenty-five miles away from Sacramento and they said,

"No."

That lets you know how much juice a Governor has against the Nuclear Regulatory Commission. The Governor of a state could say,

"This nuke here, twenty-five miles from the Capitol, is a Babcock & Wilcox exploder like the one you have over in Harrisburg, and we'd like for you to shut the sucker down until you investigate it and find out it ain't going to do that to *us*."

"No.

"No?"

"No."

"Oh. All right."

We went to Washington around then, and what we learned was that it's mostly a lot of jive going down that channel. The governmental bureaucracy is not the way to change the nukes. But the channel we can go down to help is to educate the people so that a lot of people understand it. It is not that complicated. It's a bunch of shuck and jive by the atomic scientists to make it sound like it's so complicated that the people can't have an opinion. But it's not that complicated. Most people understand it pretty good just from what everybody learned from the television and *TIME* and *Newsweek*. In that one week everybody in the United States, and the whole world, was taking a course in nuclear physics. And we've all learned enough about it to have an opinion.

I can tell you the stuff is poison, but I would really dig it better if you studied it until you understood it yourself; then you would know how it felt to you in your heart, and you would be moved to write some letters. Find out who your man is, and find out where he's at, and write him a personal letter about where he's really at. That's something anyone can do.

But really, we made our choice about the nukes a couple of years ago when we said,

"Can we take Albert and let him go full time working for Jeannine?"

Since that time it isn't just Albert; he's sucked in our whole legal crew—they're all a fine crew; I'm very proud of our lawyers. It may seem simple to us that they don't take money for what they do, but it's almost unique. You hardly find any other lawyers who do that, and that's part of why we're so strong, and why we've been able to make a difference as much as we have. Our brief in the courts is stronger than many thousands of hippies with placards in front of the nuke plant: They don't have to have anybody higher than a captain of the Highway Patrol to handle a demonstration; but we get to drag out Joseph Hendrie, Chairman of the Nuclear Regulatory Commission himself, when we take our brief to court. We're trying to educate, because the people have to understand it, to just not be run over by it.

Back in 1957, they said they were going to do Atoms for Peace, so the government decided to let private industries develop nuclear power. They gave out contracts to the corporations. And now the nuclear power industry is made up of the oil companies who bought up all the rights to that kind of stuff, and the power companies. It's like Edison Company, and Pacific Gas and Electric, and Westinghouse, and Kerr-McGee— which was an oil company, and is now the biggest uranium miners in the world, who did the mines on the Navajo reservations and are now wanting to do them in the Sioux territory in the South Dakotas. And the only thing that made any sense at all in the Washington hearings about Three Mile Island was when Kennedy and the other guys kept asking,

"When you decided to let loose some hot stuff into the atmosphere, who made the decision? Was it an Edison Company dude or was it an NRC dude?" And it had been an Edison Company dude who had made those decisions. It at least made sense that the corporation should be responsible to the Nuclear Regulatory Commission that way.

The committee hearings had the wrong actors. They had chosen them very carefully. Kennedy, with his voice and his profile, represented the Establishment position, and Hendrie was there to answer his questions. Well, that was wrong. It should have been Hendrie as head of the Nuclear Regulatory Commission, talking to Edison Company:

"Where is it at that you waited four hours to call us?

"Where is it at that you released stuff without letting us know first?

"Where is it at that we got information from the press before we got it from you?

"Why are you hiding anything from us?

"Who are you responsible to?"

Isn't that what should have been going on, and who should have been saying what to whom? They should have been regulating. That's Hendrie's gig. But he wasn't regulating; he was explaining the power company to Kennedy. It was all so incestuous it was sickening.

A private, money-making enterprise has precedence over the people. You remember when Jimmy Carter first proposed his energy program, he came on that it should be the

"Moral Equivalent of Waugh."

He really meant to put the screws on when he said it was supposed to be the moral equivalent of war, and he said everybody has to really try—the unions have to quit demanding so much money, and the businesses have to back it off, because we're messing it up. We are doing it to it. And during this year, which is the year following his heaviest speech about energy, the big businesses took in 25% profit on their investments. In some specific businesses, they took up to 42% profit, right during the middle of the recession. The oil companies took 50% and 100% and 300%; and the car companies and the electrical outfits that make televisions and appliances were jacking up the prices and gouging the people, making their profit. Well, even Jimmy doesn't like that. It probably makes him sick.

Somebody said to him, "Well, you see how much power a President has in relation to the president of a multinational corporation."

Jimmy said, "I learned that today."

The thing about the government is that they ain't squat, man. Who's doing it is the multinational corporations.

When we were up in South Dakota, John Trudell was speaking for the Sioux and for AIM. He said,

"AIM's got a bad rap because they call us communists and say we're down on the government. We're not communists. We look at the United States and Russia as two countries who are lost in industrial development and scarifying the world, just the same. And as far as being down on the goverment of the United States, we are not even down on them. Who we are down on is the multinational corporations, who owe no allegiance to any country and rape all countries equally."

He said it so true. He was so strong he nearly pasted them against the wall, but he was so true that the people gave him a standing ovation when he was done. The real truth is that the President can't do anything about the nukes, particularly. He has an opinion, he can express his opinion, but that's about the most he can do. And the only thing _we_ can really do is to educate so many people as to make the pressure come from every part of the United States and from every walk of life, and to point out that rich people get irradiated equally with poor people.

Some global problems need work. We went up to Seabrook last summer, and the governor and the local prosecutor got very nasty, threatening guns and dogs and bullets and helicopters and tactical nuclear weapons, and whatnot. They really came on like they were going to get everybody, and scared them pretty hard, because they were really afraid that they were going to get a bunch of people hurt. I don't think it was a question of the folks being afraid for themselves, afraid they would get bit by a dog or something. I think it was fear on the part of the organizers about getting people hurt. The organizers didn't feel good about putting people into a situation where they were going to get hurt. So they backed down to the point of making an agreement that they wouldn't occupy the site illegally. The same day they had the demonstration, old governor Meldrim Thompson had a clambake, with steamed clams and pictures of the governor serving steamed clams. That and the Clamshell Alliance being wiped out in the same day was just too much. He was much hipper, media-wise, than anybody else on the scene who was doing it.

After we left there, we came down to the Bronx center and we just happened to luck out that evening and catch a documentary on Greenpeace, which is the whale people. They went out to hassle the Russian fleet. They had little rubber boats with an outboard motor on them. And those big whale boats have a hole in the stern big enough to drag a whale up in. They ran their rubber boats up in it. They're stopping the whaling, too. One of our radio operators, Stephen Skinner, is on board the _Rainbow Warrior_, which has been interrupting the Icelandic whaling fleet in its coastal whaling.

I am encouraged that they shut down the Seabrook plant. I am encouraged that anybody's paying any attention at all. But it was a coincidence that there was a demonstration going on when they closed Seabrook. Demonstrations do not move nuclear regulatory commissions directly. They may move the press and the legislators, and the legislators may create a climate that may create the kind of government which moves nuclear regulatory commissions, but even though there were people sitting outside demonstrating at the time they decided to shut it down, those people outside didn't make them decide to do that. In a sense, they had to do that *in spite of* those people sitting outside. And the plant has since reopened.

I'm glad we got out without anybody hurt, because I think that prosecutor would have hurt somebody; but I also think that it's those peoples' privilege to decide that for themselves. I'm grateful that the alliance concept has been figured out, and been spread across the country and caught on. It's a good thing, in that sense; I think it's one of the strongest things happening right now.

The question of what went down at Seabrook was not the question of exactly whether or not that you sat there and got arrested or not. It's that the governor got to define what violence and non-violence were, which was a strategic error which Gandhi would not have made; that's why we miss him so much. He didn't make that particular kind of strategic error. He always kept at the forefront the moral question of who was right and who was wrong and what was going on in the situation. He didn't go get hit in the head just for the fun of it. On several occasions, he allowed himself to be smuggled out of places rather than to just be wasted on the way—because he had something else to do and didn't have time to recuperate right now or something; but when it came to the question of defining who is violent and who isn't violent and questions like that, he put his body on the line about it.

But the way the governor was talking about it, it sort of got spoken into the record that when his dog bites me I'm being violent, and that's too crazy to let pass. There should be a lot more noise about that.

At Seabrook, the D.A. and the governor used intimidating tactics to get their way. They shook their fists at those demonstrators, saying,

"You better not demonstrate on this property."

Well, what the demonstrators are supposed to do is call a press conference at the nuclear site. Really. And walk out on the nuclear site in front of all the press and say,

"Look at the way the company goons knock me down. Observe. These people are using intimidating tactics." Do it out in public. In the Sixties in Chicago, where they were beating people up and hauling them away, the demonstrators were chanting,

"The whole world is watching. The whole world is watching." You'd better believe it.

And it's not just radiation that's poisoning the biosphere. There's the chemicals, also. Monsanto and Stauffer and Hooker. Hooker is about the number one polluter in the country, and we have a Hooker representative right nearby. They're the ones who did the Love Canal at Niagara, where the dogs that went around sniffing in the vacant lots got sores in their noses that didn't heal. There was so much bad stuff in the dirt that it boiled up and destroyed their tissue. And there's a lot of chemical dumping still going on. And, as far out in the country as we are, when they cook that potash fertilizer over at Stauffer, certain radioactive stuff goes down. One byproduct is polonium-210, an alpha-emitter, and that stuff gets loose. Some of the reasons smokers get cancer is from the polonium-210 in the fertilizer which gets in the tobacco.

What can we do about all that? One thing is to try as much as possible to go organic in our entire lifestyle, so we don't have to use that kind of stuff. We can avoid buying chemicals. We can try to produce the stuff we need ourselves.

We can try not to use too much energy. And that's part of what Carter's trying to do, is to encourage conservation. But they're having an arms race in hair dryers. Hair dryers have got up to 1500, 2000 watts, besides burning up asbestos off the insulation and giving you cancer. When the Farm Band had the most speakers and Walter had two stacks of fours for his guitar and two Marshall amps, and the biggest setup we ever had onstage, that was a total of about 2000 watts, and they're putting out 2000 watts in a hairdryer. Jimmy ain't getting no respect.

Alternative sources of energy are another solution. The big companies say you can't do it, because they're trying to discourage everybody from doing it. And the way to circumnavigate that is to be decentralized. Every time you do something in your house, every time you convert your hot water heater to solar or wood, every time you figure out a more efficient way to run your energy, that's decentralized power.

One of the issues in Gandhi's time was that they were taking raw cotton from India, shipping it to England, manufacturing it, making the cloth, and shipping it back to India to sell to the people. And Gandhi said,

"It is more efficient to have a spinning wheel in every house, when you get right down to it." It's a lower level of technology, doesn't cost as much, no pollution, it's actually more economical. And there's a bunch of stuff that could be more economical for us to do it, even if it's a bit of a trip to do.

Our passive solar system at the new school on the Farm has been getting a lot of good publicity. It's miraculous that we are the ones to finally get it together to do that, as poor as we are and as close to the bone as we live, that we should be the ones who can afford to put one out and take the risk. All those big construction companies could build beautiful solar rigs. Tomorrow. They could put them up really fast, if they wanted to. But they're afraid of the economic factor. They're afraid that somebody might think they look funny, they're afraid they might not sell easy, afraid that people would be superstitious about some kinds of bugs in them. They don't do it because they're doing it from the profit factor; so it falls to the likes of us to do that sort of thing. Well, God bless our efforts. I'm really grateful to be with such inventive and creative people.

Another way to help is if anyone has any connections with anybody. We've published two books, *Honicker vs. Hendrie* and *SHUTDOWN!* If you read those and be a good student, you'll learn more than most folks you'll ever run into will know. It's a tremendous amount of information, and if you just teach yourself the nature of the trip a little bit, you'll be able to speak intelligently, and then you'll start your own kit—and when you go and argue with other folks, you'll learn a new fact now and then and get a good scary tidbit to use.

Here's a scary tidbit. If you took a fuel rod out of a nuclear reactor that had already been used, a spent fuel residue, and set it on the ground and walled over and stood by it, you would receive a lethal dose in two seconds. Now, if you took all the rods out of a reactor and stacked them in a stack and you rode by that stack on a motorcycle at 90 miles an hour, it would kill you. When you went by it, it would kill you. This is hard gamma radiation. This is why they build those four-foot-thick concrete containment vessels around it, which aren't strong enough.

When those government scientists say that there is no cancers possible from the spill at the Three Mile Island plant, what they are predicting is that not one of those particles will ever cross with anyone. I do not believe they can make that statement. I think any mathematician would laugh at that prediction, if he wasn't sold out.

So when you look at the atomic question, it's not just a trade-off between coal and uranium. It's not just a question of whether a coal-fired gasifier plant costs more or less than a nuclear plant. It's not a question of whether the United States is going to be able to stay heavy in the energy racket in comparison to other countries. It's really a question of,

Can the people of this country become educated fast enough to become wise enough to take the lead in the world in shutting them down for the sake of everyone on the planet, and everything that lives on the planet, from now and forever on.

The Hope of the World

Whenever someone stumbles on to the essential secret of the Universe, they'll always try to record it in some fashion, like sending a note to themselves knowing that they're going to lose their mind, and hoping to send themselves a note that will remind them who they are when they find it again. So we are all here remembering ourselves, or forgetting ourselves, or whatever it is we're doing. What are we doing? Why are we doing this? Sometimes the Farm seems like a great burden for each one of us to drag along—and sometimes the Farm is the note you wrote yourself to remind you who you are when you forgot again. You can't write that note on a piece of paper. You can't write it in a language, because you don't know who you're going to be, so it can't be anything just local that you write that down in; it has to be in some kind of a language that you'll be able to understand no matter how you land.

Sometimes we're a town, sometimes we're a school, sometimes we're a church, sometimes we're a little country. But we're trying to understand the One, and we're trying to understand the Many; and it's hard, as we struggle back to the One, to understand why the One would ever want to be the Many. Sometimes we stumble around here in life like someone who's taken a heavy psychedelic and has forgotten how they got that way. And they say,

"How did I get this way?"

"Oh. You mean I did this on purpose. Oh, far out. I'm supposed to be learning something from this if I did this on purpose, maybe. I wonder why I could have done this."

I look at the Farm sometimes in sort of a statistical way, like looking at graphs or something, and I say it's got to shape up. We have to do this, that, this Farm's got to shape up, got to get it together, . . . and then I go out and I look around for folks who ain't doing it, and people hardly have time to talk to me, because they're all working. When we first came here, we thought we should make it a firm policy that everybody should work at least one day a week. Why are we doing this? What are we doing this for?

I hope this isn't too pretentious an answer, but it comes really from my deepest, deepest heart and I have to say it, even at the risk of sounding foolish. We are doing this because it's the hope of the world. The mainstream culture is far wrong and has lost the essential human values, and we're trying to grow a little culture of those essential human values. It's like having one Asian Flu virus and trying to raise the whole flu off of it.

There are people just like us all around the world, people who would live here if they could, who would put their weight and strength behind this. Some of them can't get out because they're too poor; some of them couldn't get out if they had the money. Some of those countries just don't allow you to go out much.

Our obligation to those folks is not because we are braver or smarter than they are, but because we are fortunate, blind, dumb, lucky. We happen to have been thrown into a fertile field where we can grow, and we have an obligation to all those seeds that were thrown in all those places where they couldn't grow because the ground was too rocky or the government too mean. So living here is not an individual thing; in that sense, the Farm belongs to everybody. We belong to everybody.

We have a field where we hold our July celebration. Some folks might think that's a square holiday for a lot of hippies to celebrate, but I think of it as Independence Day. And it means something especially since I've traveled in a few Crown colonies, like Canada and Australia. It really means something to have never had a revolution of independence. Living in a country like this, that is as square and dumb and rich as this country is, you'd almost think that the independence gained two hundred years ago didn't mean anything because we were already so fat, square and dumb and rich that we were the shame of the world for it. But nonetheless, to have independence and to not be paying lip service to any hereditary royalty, is a grand step in mankind's evolution, and worth it. Even if we are a bunch of dumb squares in this country. And there is something about that spirit that has to continue.

The concept of independence is interesting. Some people think that independence means you don't have to take no crap off anybody. I know what it means: It means that one is sure, if one is independent, that one is not a burden on one's brothers. Independent and interdependent.

What is required is courage. And courage is one of the easier ones. It's not like you go into a situation where you are essentially weak of heart and afraid and somehow by a great effort of will you screw up your courage to overcome your cowardice to do this thing, even though it is scaring the pants off of you while you are doing it—that ain't how it works. Courage comes from "heart"— _coeur_ in French, _corazon_ in Spanish—and courage means you see the importance of this thing in front of you so strong and so seriously and you have so much heart and you care about it so much that you are single-mindedly intent on doing it, and you don't even consider whether you are afraid or not. If your knees are knocking together like castanets, it doesn't matter, because what has to be done has to be done and you don't consider that other stuff. You love somebody enough, or you love everybody enough, that it is worth your while to do it.

Heavy events like that can be initiations. You might protect yourself from life in such a way that nothing might happen to you for forty years, and then you might be walking through the park and unguardedly open your heart to someone for a second and it can go _pscchhh bang! crash!_ and completely blow your thing and have one of those initiations. That's why people sometimes have such big crying fits when they have initiations like that: "Oh, I haven't had one of those for twenty years. What have I been doing?"

What you put your attention on will prosper and grow, whether it be a way or a trade or a factory or yourself, or whether it be a giant multinational corporation. What you put your attention on will prosper and grow and be amplified; so if you have a bad self-concept, thinking you're not worth anything or that you ain't very good or that you're so leaky you're never going to be any use or that here-I-am-trying-to-do-this-for-fifteen-years-and-barely-making-a-dent-at-it or all that stuff, that's like if you had a zit and you were always up in the mirror picking at it until you pick it up into a big, red thing, from someting that only you noticed in the first place when you went to the mirror, and turned it into something everyone can see. That's like putting your attention on a fault. If someone is always sitting around saying,

"Oh, I got this problem, man, I'm so paranoid, I'm really afraid something's going to happen to me, I'm being so weird, I'm being so paranoid . . ." then they are paying attention to being paranoid. 90% of people's troubles will go away by themselves if you don't pay any attention to them.

Immanent God

There's been an idea of God that I've been woking on in my mind for years. When I was in the penitentiary, doing work release at Vanderbilt Divinity School, they talked about transcendent God and the Immanent God. And they said that a transcendant God was one that was someplace else, like—I hesitate to say the *Christian* religious concept of God, but the ordinary *American* religious concept of God—this old gentleman in this curly white beard in the other room that's got a one-way mirror that's looking into here, and you'd better not mess up or you'll get zapped.

I think that viewpoint is what's given religion a bad name in our generation; and it explains why we're having to recover all that respect for religion that used to be accorded to it automatically. Anyway, that was the transcendent God.

The immanent concept of God, they say, is a completely pagan, pantheistic one: God's in everything. They say that God can't be in everything. You can't say that God is equally in the blade of grass as he is anywhere else, because then where's your gentleman in the white suit? Where's your personal God? Who do you pray to? Is there somebody who cares about you? Does the Universe care?

Another thought coming down along this line is something I learned on my early trips. I ran into some of Einstein and I really loved him a lot. I saw what a courageous and dedicated mind he was, and I particularly liked the idea of relativity, which at that time expressed itself to me in one of those Haight Street axioms,

You can't get anywhere you can't get back from.

There was a very great deal of comfort in that. That's basic general relativity, and so I let it go at that, because it worked good for me. Then, some years later, I bumped into Bucky, and Bucky wanted, as was his way, to break that relativity down into its parts, to see what made it work. So he said it was a Universe of a single integrity composed of non-simultaneously occurring events. He said you could have a whole, one thing made up out of events that did not occur at the same time, but that all nonetheless related. It's like rope fibers: you can make a rope hundreds of yards long out of fibers three inches long—they all relate, and there's an integrity through there. Pull on one end of the rope and there's a pull on the other end. The Universe is one whole, complete thing; and even though those events are non-simultaneously occurring, it's difficult to question their reality.

There's a structure to those non-simultaneously occurring events, and that structure's sort of slopped over into the theory I've been working on all these years, about the immanent God and the transcendent God. I realized that the intelligence of God is composed of non-simultaneously occurring thoughts, and that that intelligence is as self-evidently real as the rest of the Universe in front of us, and that that structure is a way in which that immanent and that transcendent God are blended into one whole—and it's a nice machine. It will do what both sides say it will do. It will talk to you in your face, and it will follow what Jesus said, that,

"When you cleave the wood, I am inside there; when you break open the rock, I am inside there."

You have the problem posed right there. You have a transcendent character telling you he was immanent. And if we could let go of small and petty and linguistic and cultural and nationalistically-based concepts of God, we could recognize that consciousness of God is the non-simultaneously occurring intelligence linking back through time like the fibers of a rope, back to the first time anyone ever thought anything, back to the Primordial Buddha, the Alpha—and we are that. We are that. We could even say that the intelligence of God is composed of ordinary men, women and kids, thinking enlightened thoughts.

Synchronicity is another concept that is useful in understanding the mind. Carl Gustav Jung uses synchronicity in talking about the Universe; it's the basis for his using the *I Ching* at all. He says it's one of the factors in the Universe that is so delicate that you blow it by pointing it out; so I often let it go. The other end of it is that I hate to let it go: Any time it happens, I really want to make it strong, so it knows it's working good. But it's very nice the number of times, if you just pay close attention, that just about when you were thinking you wanted a drink, someone brought you one. Just watch that: Look around, and pretty soon you'll see that there's a great deal of cooperation that goes on among us, which we don't even talk about, most of the time. It is all part of the telepathic matrix of our free will.

In an issue of the Farm newspaper, _Amazing Tales of Real Life,_ someone pointed out that _love cannot compel._ You have to be free to respond to love. Any idea of God with man-sized identities and man-sized self-concepts and man-size emotions and druthers and angers and will, is all much too small. God is not mad at any of us. God ain't mad. We ain't mad. We're part of God. How can God be radically different from our best and highest Self? How would we recognize God if we didn't have it in ourselves?

You have to be really careful in your concept of God, because once you start ascribing man-sized things to God, you get yourself in a position of maybe you ought to jump off on a Holy War because God's so mad at these folks that maybe you ought to get with God and act with Him and jump off and have a war on these folks. The concept of the Holy War is one of the most terrible things that has ever happened to humankind, and one of the most unreligious. Holy War is like saying,

"Light Dark,"or

"Up Down."

A lot of the reason that intelligent people are offended by religion is that they get into one of these anthropomorphic concepts of God, with God having a lot of druthers about stuff and pushing people around about it. People rebel at that concept of God; and if they're not given anything else, they just become intelligent agnostics and go around arguing with preachers. I argued with a preacher one time until one of his students almost punched me in the mouth before I ever thought any of that stuff was real. I got a letter about it a couple of months ago, reminding me I had been that way when they had known me.

Many books try to say that they are maps of the astral territory. But the astral territory has no map. The astral territory contains

the totality of the possibilities of imagination forever—
everything is in it. You could get anything out of it you want.

There's a dude who says he's the only master of astral travel,
that you have to come to him to learn astral travel, and if you
travel through him, you get to travel through a neat Universe he
tells you about. Well, that's his Universe out there in that astral
thing, and every other universe is equally valuable. That astral
plane is the resultant vector field of *all* our common intelligences,
and nobody can draw a map down something like that. They see
certain events and they place them in a space/time intelligence a
lot, to put it in a context they're familiar with.

Gautama Buddha started into religion because he thought the
Indian religion of the time didn't give the poor people a fair shake.
They had a locked-in caste system so that if you were born an
Untouchable, nobody touched you, and that was that; and if you
were a Brahmin, you were virtually above the law. You were born
in those positions, and they said that God had ordained that some
people have it together more than others. Even two hundred
years after the American revolution, that hits American ears
really funny. And it hit Buddha's ears funny 2,500 years ago.

On the other hand, it is self-evident that some of us are more
together than others of us, and that if you took all the people in
the world and sorted them out into those that are together and
those that are less together, you can take them and sort them out
into something that looks like the Hindu caste system. But the
trouble with that is that they would *change consciousness.* People
would *flow up and down*, and you wouldn't be able to hold it still.
People would be learning stuff and changing position, and you
could never get it organized.

There is no value in laying it out like that. We want all of our
needs, and the things with which we fulfill all those needs, to be as
decentralized and spread out as possible, without artificial
structure, and then the whole thing comes out even. So even
though you see events sometimes which may make you think of
the other-world planes as being of the same kind of plane as this
one, that if you put something there it generally stays there and
that kind of phenomenon—those planes are not that way. And it's
only in your mind that you think they are, and it limits your ability
to think, and the scope of your imagination. There's a lot of

rigidity and three-dimensionality and inertia in this plane—the laws of thermodynamics and all—but none of that stuff exists on those other planes.

One concept you find born-again Christians using is the idea of spiritual warfare, fighting between God and the devil. But that's a very recent attitude. Saint Augustine pointed out that evil has no intrinsic existence. Nothing exists without some good in it, because if it didn't have any good in it at all, it wouldn't have any existence at all. Nothing exists which is bad in its totality, or it wouldn't exist. For God is all.

You can see how dichotomy-thinking gets you in trouble. If you can decide that it's God and the devil, you can decide its the Capitalists and the Communists right on top of that, and you can run your whole lifestyle right down that path, until you find yourself having to duke it out with somebody. Then you've taken all of the hidden, subtle, artistically-distributed dichotomies in the world, and broken them all down into something you have to fight.

I love telepathic phenomena, but I've _never_ been to a seance or anything like that. It seems so slow and pedestrian and dull to try to set up such a Mickey-Mouse thing like that, when if you just wander around and pay attention, somebody will do something that will blow your mind every little while—if you're just paying attention.

Actually, the way our culture's knowledge is put together, you have to say that any case of telepathy is miraculous. The world view of the materialistic universe up until Haight-Ashbury times was pretty locked up about telepathy; Dr. Rhine over at Duke University was reduced to making little decks of cards and dealing them off and having people guess the cards, and having them do it thousands of times, and running it through his computer backwards and sideways and upside down for all the different correlations, to see if he could find telepathy way out there in some decimal place that he could prove, because the world view was so against it: No Miracles Allowed. He had to do it out at the seventeenth decimal place; they wouldn't just let him pull off a miracle.

And now there have been too many of us who have had too many weird things happen to ever be put back in that box again, and *that* is miraculous. There are thousands and millions of people in inner cities and places like that who don't know that yet. It's so miraculous that we get to know it, and get to know it so commonly, so everyday that we forget that there are whole cultures where they're just bashing their head up against a wall. In Detroit, in New York, there are really heavy trips going down, and nobody thinks it's heavy or has the nerve to say it's anything but dog-eat-dog. Anybody who says it's anything other than dog-eat-dog is considered feeble-minded. In those cultural contexts it is miraculous to know that it's not that way. Darwin and his theories of competition notwithstanding.

It also helps to cultivate a light touch and a sense of humor. Having weathered a few disasters really helps. If you've seen it when it's *really* hit the fan a few times, you really appreciate boredom.

Religious teachers and commentators have been funnier than most people realize. The story in *Zen Flesh, Zen Bones*—where the dude goes in to talk to the Zen master and the Zen master throws him out and slams the door on his leg on the way out and the dude becomes enlightened at that point—is a very funny story. It's also like *The Diamond Sutra* when Buddha says to Subhuti,

"Subhuti, have I spoken to you of these grains of sand?"

He's just been on one of these incredible grains-of-sand trips, grains of sand countless as the worlds of galaxies, countless into the expanding . . . and he says,

"Subhuti, have I spoken to you of these grains of sand?"

And Subhuti is so loyal that he doesn't even give him a hard time for that; he just says,

"Yes, you have spoken of these grains of sand."

It's very dry, but it's very funny.

Mind at Play

You can have a vision where you realize that you are one of the Buddhas, and that everybody is one. Everybody is one, and you are one of them. It doesn't devalue it because everybody else is one, too. It's not like, *Aww, everybody else is, too.* It's like, *Thank God no one is left out. Praises be that no one is left out.*

Then you can have a vision where you can feel like you're the All. It depends on what level you look at it from. If you look at it from the material plane, you are obviously *not* the all—there's Pittsburgh, which is outside of you. But the truth of that lies in the vision plane, because you *can* be the All in the vision plane. So if someone has a vision that they're part of the All, you can't put them down, because it can be true in the vision plane.

You can also decide you are the truth body of the Buddha—or you can have an experience of being truth. This is a very heavy trip. This is one where your sanity really gets tested. You have to let truth happen. You can't be attached to knowing truth. It's easier to *be* truth than it is to *know* truth. You have to be real careful that the opinions you have had *since* you had that vision don't become truth to you. If you had that vision, that was the truth; but it does not guarantee that everything you think *after* that is truth. And having been part of the All does not mean that since you are part of the All, that it doesn't matter what you do, and you can do anything to the other people because they're just extras in your movie.

That's what a heresy is: When you make a mistake in religious thought that makes it so you can go out and hurt people or you can do something that's obviously irreligious. Heresy is the exit gate out of sanity. It's not something that's arbitrarily decided. Most heresies are self-evident. Obviously, having had an experience of the All does not mean that you are the landlord of the All, and can do anything you want to to the All.

Sometimes we have realizations of one kind or another, and it makes a tremendous difference how you *do* that. I know a lot of people came in here banged and crazy in such directions that may have been personally very exotic, but actually, we'd have four or five avatars hit the Gate in a week, sometimes. Different religions—Jesuses and Buddhas, Thorazines and Zoroastrians and whatnot. And a lot of us who are here now are those people, and remember coming in the Gate in that condition. And we didn't forget that trip. We still remember it; we just don't push it on our friends so hard.

It doesn't make you able to change the truth, because the truth is the truth, regardless of what you do to it; so if you think that you have become Truth and you can change Truth, *you is wrong.*

Truth stays the same, like a clear spring, for everyone who drinks from it, it's the same spring, and someone doesn't come along and change it all of a sudden.

All of this is about a technology of the mind, and about energy. When we're going down the road in the Greyhound, we're making seventy miles an hour, weighing twenty tons, almost 40,000 pounds—that is a kind of energy. You can study about that kind of energy in high school. It's called kinetic energy. All of the inertia that it took to get it to that speed, is stored as it rolls.

At the same time, we're thinking—there is mind at play. And we have another kind of energy happening, another kind of energy that's as obvious and as real as the inertia of that twenty tons of Greyhound. You cannot say that mind at play is not real. But somehow we do not understand, perhaps, how to mix, and how to create an equation where you can take the energy of the bus, that stored kinetic power, and the energy of those minds, and create an equation that has both those forms of energy expressed in it. It should be possible, since we know from our own personal exerience that those are both real forms of energy.

In algebra, they often throw in another factor that can have something common to both. I think the common factor in this equation is attention. We say attention is energy, and both of these can be considered in terms of attention. What keeps the inertia of that seventy mile-an-hour, 40,000 pounds, in a condition of existence, is the attention of the driver. If his attention should wander for even a couple of seconds, all that energy would expend itself—somehow. It's held in place in a very tenuous, delicate web of connecting factors. All of the work that's gone into the design of the bus, all of the repair jobs that have been done to the bus, all culminate in the phenomenon where the driver's attention, plus the bus, creates a receptacle for energy. And the driver's attention is a function of mind at play. He got into the same level that way. And you can see that at the level of energy, something that seems ephemeral when you consider the energy of that 40,000 pounds of Greyhound moving seventy miles an hour, is maintaining and controlling, and in some fashion being more powerful, or a _higher form of energy_ than that 40,000 pounds of Greyhound moving. _Mind at play._